THE LAKES

THE LAKES

NORMAN NICHOLSON

ILLUSTRATED AND WITH MAP

ROBERT HALE · LONDON

First published 1963 as *Portrait of the Lakes*. Reprinted 1964 and 1965. Revised edition 1972.

This edition first published 1977

ISBN 0 7091 6246 4 (*paperback*)
ISBN 0 7091 2897 5 (*hardcover*)

Robert Hale Limited
Clerkenwell House
Clerkenwell Green
London EC1

Printed in Great Britain by
Jarrold and Sons Ltd, Norwich

CONTENTS

ILLUSTRATIONS

ACKNOWLEDGEMENTS

Illustrations 1, 4, 7, 11, 14, 15, 24 and 25 were taken by
Derek Widdicombe; 3 by Reece Winstone; 6 by W.
Wilson; 17, 20, 22 and 23 by John Edenbrow; 18 by J.
Hardman; 19 and 21 by E. Hector Kyme; and the
remaining ones by R. C. Morton.

ACKNOWLEDGEMENTS
to the First Edition, 1963

My grateful acknowledgements are due to the many people who have helped me both with this book and for my previous studies of the Lake counties. In particular I want to mention Mr. J. C. Hobbs and Mr. J. Melville (both of Barrow Naturalists' Society), Mr. W. Wilson and Mr. Frank Warriner, the late Miss M. C. Fair and the late Canon S. Taylor—all of whom have given me help, advice and encouragement over many years.

I should also like to thank Mr. R. E. O. Pearson who has read part of this book in manuscript, and Mr. Lionel Butterworth and Mr. Walter Sansom, each of whom has allowed me to study work he has carried out on special aspects of the history of Furness. Also, the late Mr. Philip Cleave, Mr. George Bott, Mr. and Mrs. Delmar Banner and Mr. Otto Secher, who have given me help and information on specific matters. Also, Mr. J. Scott, Mr. J. Boyle, and Mr. R. B. Davis, who allowed me to visit the local industries and taught me much about them.

I must mention, too, with particular gratitude, the willing assistance so often given by Mr. A. Davies of Millom Public Library, Mr. K. Smith of Carlisle City Library, and Mr. D. Hay of Whitehaven Public Library, together with that of the Librarian and staff of the Cumberland County Library.

Finally, I wish to thank Miss C. Mullins, who has performed what many of my friends regard as the almost impossible feat of typing this manuscript without any previous knowledge of my handwriting, and also my wife who has taken me by car to many parts of this district which otherwise I might never have been able to see.

N.N.

This map is reproduced with permission from the Ordnance Survey

I

THE LAY-OUT

I LIVE in the Lake District. Not on a fell-side farm or in a remote dale cottage, but in the main shopping street of a town of nearly ten thousand inhabitants. Yet, when I look from my bedroom window across a huddle of roofs and aerials, I can see rock country only about a mile and a half away. In autumn the larches burn through green-yellow to brown-purple behind the haze of the town smoke. In spring the first unpacking of the bracken is as obvious from two thousand yards as it would be at a distance of two feet. In summer, when the cows climb to the crest of the hill during the hot nights, each single beast can be seen, neat as a ladybird, in the morning light. Behind the hill, only two miles further away, is the hulk of a fell visible in clear weather from both South Scotland and Wales. And further round, if I lean out of my window, I can see the sky-line of the central fells—Scafell, Scafell Pike, Great End, Harter Fell, Bowfell, Crinkle Crags, Coniston Old Man—an horizon unsurpassed in England. No one, surely, could doubt that this is the true district of the Lakes.

Yet, if I go round to the back of my house, I get another view. For now, closer than the rocks at the front, are the cliffs of a slag-bank, and bigger than the trunks of the larches are the chimney-stacks of old furnaces. And only a little further away are the pit-shafts and spoil-heaps of an iron mine and a cargo-pier jutting out into the estuary. This, many people would say, is not the Lake District at all.

But they would be wrong. For the furnaces used to smelt Lake District ore with Lake District limestone, and the town itself is built of Lake District slate and Lake District flags. The men of the town, to a large extent, come from the same stock as the men of the dales, and they speak the same kind of language. As with the hill-farmer, the shepherd or the quarryman, their life has grown out of the rock. Their work once came from the rock, and they live roofed, walled and pavemented by rock like dwellers in caves. Every bit as much as the water-ousel and the Herdwick sheep they can claim to belong to the Lake Region of Cumberland, Westmorland and North Lancashire.

The extent of this region is fairly easy to define. Its western boundary is the coast, from Workington to Carnforth; its eastern boundary, either the A6 road over Shap, or a line sweeping along the valleys of the Lune and the Eden to include the fells of east Westmorland. The northern boundary begins at Penrith, bulges round the back of the Caldbeck Fells, and joins the route of the old Keswick to Workington railway at Cockermouth. Inside this area there is much variety. The centre is a mountain dome, sliced with valleys, rocky or half barren. Where the valleys open out into the wider lowlands, we find the tourist villages and at least one important manufacturing centre, the town of Kendal. The Cumberland sector of the coastline is almost unindented, while the Lancashire sector is nothing but indentations—the long estuaries, sands and salt-flats of Morecambe Bay, where the sea is often lost sight of altogether except at the highest point of the tide. Near the coast there are also the two important industrial areas of West Cumberland and Furness, with the coal, steel and shipbuilding towns of Workington, Whitehaven and Barrow.

On a map the area seems to have an obvious physical unity, for you see a cartwheel pattern of lakes and valleys, with the hub somewhere about Dunmail Raise. But this physical unity, oddly enough, has a dis-uniting effect on the people who live in the Lakes. For the hub is not a gathering-point but a point of departure. Two people living twenty miles apart on opposite sides of the hub might be a hundred miles apart as far as social life is concerned. Each dale is divided from the rest by high ridges. There are passes and tracks which were never an obstruction to the energetic, and today there are roads which are no obstruction to cars. But, by a long tradition, the life of the dales does not leapfrog from one dale to another over the intervening ridges: it flows up and down the valleys. Like the becks it begins at the dale-head, gathers tributaries from farms and hamlets, and descends to the comparative lowlands where it usually finds a village or small town to act as warehouse, post office and bus-station. Towns of this kind are Keswick, Ambleside, Cartmel, Coniston, Broughton-in-Furness and Gosforth. Beyond the inner ring of small towns is a further ring of larger ones, where contact is made between the dales and the farming or industrial lowlands. Such

towns are Penrith, Appleby, Kendal, Ulverston, Whitehaven and Cockermouth, some of which have become industrialized though they still carry out their old function of market town for the surrounding district. In fact, the social life of the dales tends to diverge to the periphery of a large circle. In most rural areas the life of the countryside flows to one central town or group of towns. Here it is just the other way round.

How greatly the mountains divide the people who live among them can be seen from the case of the two Seathwaites. Both are dale villages. From one to the other is less than ten miles as the raven flies and even to men the route by Esk Hause and Moasdale, though rough, is not much further. But one Seathwaite is in Borrowdale, which runs due north, and the other is in Dunnerdale, which runs south. The farmer's wife in Borrowdale does her shopping in Keswick; her next-dale neighbour beside the Duddon goes down to Broughton, and beyond to Ulverston or Barrow. Barrow and Keswick are not widely separated to anyone with a car, but, until recently, the dalesman did not often own a car, and if he tried to make the journey by rail, he would have been lucky to manage it in four hours.

Yet in spite of all these barriers and divisions, the lake areas of Cumberland, Westmorland and North Lancashire form a true whole. At one time they formed almost a small, separate, self-contained kingdom, locked off both from England and Scotland. This was partly due to the common Norse ancestry of the people, and partly to the character of the land, which imposed upon them a peculiar and uniform way of life. From about the tenth century onward there grew up in the dales a group of small communities, poor, austere, largely self-subsistent and always self-reliant. Even when the Industrial Revolution opened up the mining districts of West Cumberland and Furness, the same tradition persisted, for mining had been known there for 2,000 years, and in any case, the new industrial towns of the nineteenth century were almost as isolated from the rest of England as were the Lakes.

So the dalesman and the miner remained on terms one with another, and one man would often shift from farm to mine and back again as work was offered. Whitehaven and Keswick belonged and still belong to the same geographical unit and both, in the first place, were mining towns. It is easy to understand why the National Park should omit the industrial towns of the west

Black Combe from Whicham Valley (Skiddaw Slate)

from the area it controls, but to pretend that they do not really belong to the Lake District is mere tourist-minded, urban snobbery.

The Two Cartwheels

It was Wordsworth who first compared the pattern of ridges and dales to a cartwheel. He noticed, also, that the system really falls into the shape of two cartwheels, separated by the north to south geological fault in which lie Thirlmere, Grasmere, Rydal Water and Windermere. The hub of the western wheel is on Esk Hause; that of the eastern, on Helvellyn. Perhaps, the most satisfactory image for the western system, however, is that of a lemon-squeezer, with the dales gouged out of the dome and sloping radially to the rim.

If, now, you imagine that the right side of the squeezer, as you hold it in your hand, has been broken off, then you will get something of the effect of the Thirlmere-Windermere fault. For on that side of the dome the dales are all cut short. Easedale and the two Langdales break off into Windermere, while the little valleys on the south-eastern slope of Wetherlam and Coniston Old Man turn into Yewdale and Coniston Lake. But through the whole of the western semi-circle, from Keswick in the north to Millom in the south, the dales radiate in regular order: Borrowdale, the Buttermere-Crummock-Lorton valley, Ennerdale, Wasdale, Eskdale and Dunnerdale, with smaller dales like Newlands, Miterdale, and the valleys of the Calder and the Bleng, to fill up the cracks, or, rather, to make minor grooves between the major ones. The eastern cartwheel, which lies largely in Westmorland, is much less complete. It has two major dales, Patterdale and Mardale, both of which lie north-east. Westward there are only the gills which run to the Thirlmere fault. To the south, the Troutbeck valley flows into Windermere, while to the south-east a number of smaller valleys (Kentmere, Longsleddale and Bannisdale) find their way eventually to the course of the River Kent.

The main lines of communication, by road and railway, enclose both these cartwheels in a rough, bulging circle, of which the four corners, if one may call them so, are Whitehaven, Barrow, Kendal and Penrith. Across the diameter of the circle there is no railway, but a road runs from Keswick to Ambleside, by the Thirlmere-Windermere trough, over Dunmail Raise. For two centuries this has been the main trans-Lakes thoroughfare for the tourist, but lately it is being used more and more by heavy traffic as an alternative to Shap (chiefly in winter) or to the tedious west-coast route round the inlets of Morecambe Bay. To find huge, industrial lorries charging along the shore of Thirlmere or Rydal, or within a few yards of Dove Cottage, is obviously ridiculous, and shows how road-policy has so far failed either to preserve the Lakes or to serve the industry of West Cumberland.

The eastern cartwheel is bisected by the main road from Patter-dale over Kirkstone Pass into Troutbeck and Windermere. But until recently, the western one could not be crossed except by foot, though the passes of Honister and Newlands and roads over Cold Fell and Birker Moor all cut off considerable corners. Today, however, the route from Ambleside to the west coast is open to cars—by Little Langdale, Wrynose Pass, Hardknott Pass and Eskdale. Hardknott is the most severe test that faces any motorist in the district, but the surface is good, and the road takes you through country hardly seen, at one time, by any but the most adventurous tourist. Even today, in the journey from Little Langdale Tarn to The Woolpack Inn in Eskdale, there is scarcely a roof, a wall, or a post that differs from what might have been seen by the travellers of the eighteenth century. Only the tarmac is new, and that is not conspicuous. But what a difference it makes, for even when no car is in sight—which, in the holiday months is not often—the loneliness, the remoteness, is gone.

Yet perhaps on an October evening, with the dusk gathering above the river gravel and the mist clotting in the V of the pass, the bracken sodden and brown and the bitter-orange fruits of bog asphodel rotting into the mosses—perhaps, then, you can sense something of the almost Icelandic isolation in which the people of these dales once lived.

The Shap Route

From the Ice Age almost to the present day the Lakes have remained divided and isolated—a difficult spot to get about in and a difficult spot to get *to*. They were also, and still are, a diffi-cult spot to get past, for until 1971 there were only two ways of circumventing them, except by going as far east as Yorkshire.

The first was by Shap—the more familiar route to outsiders and one of great historical importance. Prince Charles marched this

way in 1745 and afterwards retreated, followed by the Duke of
Cumberland. For many years it was the main route from England
to Scotland, both by road and rail. The road, on the Kendal side,
swings up through rounded, bouncing, deeply-dented, Pennine-
like country, and descends to Shap village down a featureless,
even slope, scratched and dusted by limestone quarries and
cement-works, like a vast concrete ramp only half-overgrown
with weed. According to the map it lies entirely in the county of
Westmorland, but it is really a segment of Birmingham or Glasgow drawn into a long moving chain. Yet from a café window or
from a lorry-driver's cabin you can look down into clefts and
dales and hamlets scarcely ever visited by a stranger—places compared to which the better-known Lake District valleys are like
little Blackpools or Piccadillies.

In the winter Shap used to be the most dangerous lorry-trap in
England. It probably gets less snow than Bowes Moor, between
Brough and the Great North Road, but it is open to freezing
winds, blizzards and mist, and has patches as steep as some of the
Lake passes with a dizzy drop at the edge. Lorries could lie for
days, like abandoned tanks after a military retreat, while at the
same time the roads along the coast had not even a whitening of
hoar-frost on them. In 1970, however, the M6 motorway was
extended north of Carnforth to provide an alternative to Shap,
running some miles to the east and by-passing the towns of Kendal and Penrith. The new route offers easier gradients, gentler
curves and wider carriage-ways though at the cost of making a
terrible hash of the Lune Gorge near Tebay. Moreover, some of us
suspect that the road may be nearly as exposed to snow as was
Shap. A few bad winters will bring the test.

The Coast Route

The new M6 is really a gigantic by-pass, and it is the coastal
route which is the main approach to the Lakes and has had the
greater importance in the lives of the people. But it is a very slow
route. The railway, too, offers a slow journey, with magnificent
views up the river-mouths, but also with many stops and much
doubling back and shifting of direction. A traveller going from
Ulverston to the north will find the afternoon sun shining on his
right hand when he sits facing the engine. A traveller from Millom

to the south will find, after about an hour and a half, that he is not one mile nearer London than when he set out.[1] Along the coast, between Sellafield and St. Bees, there is only a single-line track, and trains often have to wait in the little dune-side stations for other trains to pass. Many people from West Cumberland prefer to travel to London by Carlisle, and the Furness people to approach Scotland by Carnforth.

Yet for centuries the main stream of life in the district has flowed along the coast route. The Romans established a port at Ravenglass and the Norsemen arrived on that same coast. Medieval pack-horse trains passed up and down, crossing the sands of Morecambe Bay and the Duddon Estuary. In the eighteenth century, the route was regularly used by travellers on horse-back and in carriages, and as late as the middle of the nineteenth century there was a public service from Ulverston to Lancaster. Even after the railway was built, carriers continued to cross the sands bringing goods and passengers of the poorer sort. My own grandmother first came to Millom, in the 1860s, by horse and cart over the Duddon Sands from Furness. Later still, herds of cattle and sheep were brought over the Border from Scotland, or shipped to the Solway ports from Ireland, and driven along the coast to the slaughter-houses of Lancashire. Many, no doubt—cattle, sheep, horses and men—never got across. The quicksands are notorious and do not always stay in the same place. More dangerous still is the incoming tide, for the water can rise in the channels, making coils and knots round the traveller, while he remains unaware, because it is hidden from his sight in the deep, steep-sided gulleys. But once the tide has poured over the kerbs of the gulleys it can cover acres of sand or marsh in a very short time. One minute the traveller is out on a huge plain, the flat, wet sands all round, the coast far away. The low limestone rocks on the shore seem to pile themselves surprisingly high above him, wall-ing him off from the world in a huge hollow that is neither sea nor land. The tide rises an inch or two, and at once he is a mile out at sea, floundering about up to his ankles, and looking like St. Peter walking on the waters. Then, unless he is a strong swimmer, he will find it hard to get back to the shore, for the gullies and the firm sand are hard to distinguish under water. Indeed, it might be

[1] i.e. at a point between Grange-over-Sands and Arnside where the railway line lies in the same latitude as Millom.

be best for him to stay quietly on his ridge of sand and hope that the tide will turn before it rises above his neck.

Yet in spite of the danger, the crossing of the sands remained for many years by far the most popular prelude to the Lake Tour. The danger, in fact, made it still more popular, for it added adventure to the trip, helping the travellers to see the Lakes as a place apart, almost an island, remote and strange. They viewed the Bay from the ramparts of Lancaster Castle, and saw the fells arranged in an "amphitheatre"—it was a word they loved—from Black Combe round to Ingleborough. Then they embarked on the sands from Hest Bank and moved off into an amphibious, ambiguous world of mists and ripples and broken light on pools and gulleys. It was a landscape of archaic browns and greys, and the enormous glowing skies of Claude Lorraine—the kind of ideal country which the painters of two centuries had been dreaming about. When they landed on the shore they would soon come up against the hard facts of the Lake rock, yet out in the Bay they could live on in the artist's dream. An after-glow of this adventure can be caught today by those who join the cross-bay walks organized once or twice a year from Hest Bank and Grange-over-Sands.

II

THE ROCKS

At bottom the Lake District is a piece of rock. It is the rock which makes the land and the land has made the people. And even when industry came to the North-west, it came out of the rock, for it is iron and coal which made modern Cumberland and North Lancashire. The variety of the landscape, the texture of the fells, the form of the buildings and even the colour of a town street are all to be accounted to the rock. To look at the scenery without trying to understand the rock is like listening to poetry in an unknown language. You hear the beauty but you miss the meaning.

The rocks of the Lake District are of two kinds—sedimentary and igneous. If none of these had been disturbed they would have rested one on the other like the layers of a liquorice all-sort with the oldest at the bottom and the newest at the top. This order has been broken up by cracks and bucklings in the rind of the earth, by faults, landslides, earthquakes and volcanic action, and also by the wearing away of the surface by wind, rain, rivers and by ice. But geologists are able to read the order in which the rocks were made by studying the fossils preserved in them. Here, then is a table of the chief deposits of the district, arranged in the order of the geological periods to which each belongs, the youngest being at the top:

Period	Deposits
Post-Glacial:	Sand-dunes, silting up of lakes
Glacial:	Boulder clay
Permian:	St. Bees and Penrith sandstone
Carboniferous:	Coal measures
	Mountain limestone
Old Red Sandstone:	Igneous intrusions such as Eskdale Granite
Silurian:	Slates and grits of Westmorland and North Lonsdale
Ordovician:	Coniston Limestone
	Borrowdale Volcanic Series
	Skiddaw Slate

The main lay-out of these rocks is easy to remember, for the older ones are in the middle with the newer ones encircling them like rings. Thus we get a central knot of Skiddaw Slate, Borrowdale Volcanics and Silurian rocks, and round them an inner ring of limestone and an outer ring of sandstone, with a few patches of still younger rocks at the edge. They were not laid down in rings. It is more as if they had been laid in layers and then buckled into a huge dome; rain and ice peeled away the upper layers as if slicing off the top of an onion, until in the middle the lower layers were exposed, and in the outer rings, the upper layers. Such an explanation is grotesquely over-simplified, for the laying-down and peeling-away process took place more than once, with many ups and downs, shifts, slips and concertina-ings, but the general effect is more or less as I have described it.

The Older Rocks: Skiddaw Slate

The old rocks—and they are among the oldest in Europe—are harder and tougher than the newer rocks, and form the central hub of the Lake District with its spokes of ridges and dales.

The oldest of the lot is the Skiddaw Slate: a mud-rock, laid down at the delta of a river on the shores of a shallow sea. It is softer than much of the Borrowdale rocks, and though it is called a slate, it is not very slaty—that is, it does not easily split into thin slivers like roofing slate. Here and there it breaks up into small fragments and forms screes, mostly scabby and small, but on the whole the surface disintegrates into soil, so that grass can grow and heather. It wears smoothly into rounded outlines with even slopes. These rocks occupy most of the northern part of the district. Bassenthwaite, Crummock and Loweswater lie entirely in Skiddaw Slate; Derwentwater and Buttermere, almost so. Ennerdale Water and Ullswater have their lower reaches among it—though the Ullswater patch is detached from the main block. This main block includes Skiddaw itself and Saddleback; all the fells around the Newlands Valley; Grasmoor and the fells around Whinlatter and westwards to the edge of the iron ore district. There are also a few outlying patches: one in the Eden valley on Crossfell, and one in the south which includes Black Combe.

Skiddaw and Saddleback are among the most mathematically ordered of all the fells, and might have been planned by a cubist painter. Yet, at the same time, they are alive and animal. The volcanic rocks, too, are alive, but with a fantastic life, as if they were grotesque, contorted creatures of folk-lore, but the Skiddaw fells are like prehistoric monsters.

The smoothness of the rock emphazises its animal look, for instead of the patch and jigsaw texture of the craggier hills, we find an even-coloured hide of grass or bracken bulging round flanks and haunches. Saddleback does not suggest any specific animal shape, and Skiddaw is more of a pyramid—though an animal, too, as if a pyramid could turn sphinx. But Black Combe, in the south, is the Sphinx itself. Look at it from Silecroft Shore or Layriggs—the head has gone, but the chest muscles are there, the paws with a gulley between them, and the back stretching to White Combe with the ribs and the loins swelling above Whicham Valley.

Each of the Skiddaw fells has its own individuality, yet they are all of the same family. They are epic or just narrative verse rather than the dramatic poetry of the volcanic rock. Perhaps their finest and boldest effect comes from size and solidity, from sheer cubic content. Hollow out Saddleback and you would have a dish-cover that would fit over London. All the people alive on earth could easily be heaped inside it.

Moreover, many of these fells are rather isolated, so that, unlike those of the central dales, you can see them whole and separate: Skiddaw, for instance, seen from Ashness Bridge, slanting straight from top to lakeside. Most isolated of all is Black Combe, with only a bleak sprawl of moorland to join it to the Eskdale fells ten miles away. Black Combe, indeed, is well known to many who have never visited the Lakes, for it dominates the area from mid-Cumberland to mid-Lancashire even as Criffell dominates the Scottish banks of the Solway. On a summer evening, from the north pier at Blackpool, you can see a blunt-headed mountain bullocking into the green of the twilight and leaping, apparently, straight into the tide. That is Black Combe, and that is Skiddaw Slate.

Yet sometimes this rock is much less self-assertive. Back of Skiddaw, for instance, there is a great stretch of moorland curved and moulded like a dollop of clay in the hands of a sculptor—the pressure of each finger leaving a shallow valley. This is the emptiest landscape in the Lakes, without a tree, without a farm, without a wall. Whole valleys lie bare and open to the eye, with scarcely a wisp of bracken to preserve their modesty. On the roads round Uldale and Hesket Newmarket you can drive for miles without meeting another car even when the Keswick streets are as jammed as the Strand. This is the land of John Peel and of Josiah Relph, the eighteenth-century Cumberland poet, who wrote his dialect eclogues as he coughed his life away at Sebergham.

But if the Caldbeck Fells are frank and open, the Buttermere Valley is enclosed and secretive. Even at the height of the holiday season the visitor feels something of a trespasser. The valley includes two lakes, Buttermere and Crummock, together with Loweswater in a tributary side-valley, and each seems set in a roughly circular, unbroken basin. It is hard to see where the water can flow out. The fells stand round about—Mellbreak, High Stile, Fleetwith Pike, Robinson—sloping so easily from base to summit that you scarcely realize how high they are. It is only when some high-up, measurable object catches your eye—a cairn, maybe, or a bush of broom—that the mountain comes into perspective. Then you feel the mass of it towering above you like a boot above a beetle.

At Gatesgarth, beyond Buttermere, the road bears left over Honister, but this is not the true head of the dale. Bear right, at Gatesgarth, along the track that leads to Warnscale Bottom between Fleetwith Pike and Haystacks. Almost in a matter of yards you will find yourself blocked out from the world—the beck running dead-straight along the flat pavement of upland pasture. There are drains cut in the peat, and broken-down walls, and sheep with their late lambs, all in a corridor not much wider than a football pitch between the enormous prison-walls of the fells. The silence is so solid that you would need a pneumatic drill to bore through it, yet only a couple of hundred yards away the cars are trailing one another on the sharp turns of Honister.

Skiddaw Slate is of no use for roofing, yet all round you will find small quarries where stone has been taken for rough building. For throughout the Lakes, walls, barns and cottages are put together out of the material that comes most easily to hand, whether it is slate, sandstone or cobbles from the shore. The fell walls, in fact, do not look as if they had been built at all—they look as if they had grown, like the gorse or the bilberries. How they stand is a continual puzzle, for the stones are held together only by the force of gravity; no mortar and no soil. Yet they keep their footing and balance on the steepest slopes, climbing high over crags, even when there is an easy way round.

The walls often look as old as the stone circles, of the breakings of which some of them were built. Most, in fact, are not very old at all, having been piled together in the eighteenth and early nineteenth centuries when labour was cheap. Some mark a parish or a landowner's boundary; others record merely a not very successful attempt to win a few more acres from the fell. Many seem to have no purpose at all or a purpose forgotten generations ago. There is a road over Bootle Fell, from Duddon Bridge to Waberthwaite, by which the traveller can cut ten miles off the journey round the south of Cumberland. I walked it as a boy, when it was a turf track across the grey-brown moor-grass. Today there is a line of tarmac with good passing-places for cars. The road climbs and scoops through the sour, indeterminate moor—country as little worth enclosure, it would seem, as any in Cumberland. Yet just below the spot where the old Bootle Workhouse road forks off to the left, you find that you are fenced in by stone walls, so ancient, unrepaired and broken-down that they look like ruined foundations revealed in an archaeological dig. The walls begin without apparent cause—the one on your right, as you descend, keeping close to the road, the other dipping to the banks of Kinmont Beck. They come together again, accompany you on either side as far as Buckbarrow Bridge, and then fall away as inexplicably as they began. In front, or behind, is the empty fell-side, and you feel that you have been walking through a dead age.

The quarries which provided the stone for these walls do not mar the landscape in the least. From a distance they look like the scars on an old man's face; close at hand, they are as charming as any natural gill or grotto. I am thinking not of the large commercial quarries but of small fell-side pits dug to give a farmer stone to build a byre or a wall. There are scores of them, all over the district, abandoned and mostly half-full of water. Sometimes, near the farms, they are used as shelter for a fowl-house or a dump of swedes. But sometimes they are on a steep slope, so that, when one side of the quarry is level with your feet, the other is high above you, the walls sloping up and round like the shovel which grocers once used for weighing out sugar. The rock is dark and thorn trees bend over it, making it darker still. It may be quite bare or it may be festooned like the Hanging Gardens of Babylon with spleenworts and lichen and hairy bittercress. If the quarry is open to the sun, there may be the white buttercup flowers of crowfoot floating on the water or even Grass of Parnassus in the mud. If there is soil on the ledges, there may be the bush-like tutsan, or St. John's-wort, the fruit of which begins as a bright yellow bead and ripens to almost black. And even if there seems to be no soil at all, there will still be brambles, clinging on, black-green or red, throughout the winter. In such quarries you can see that even Skiddaw Slate has its slight variations of colour, being sometimes just dull grey, and having sometimes a purplish or a yellowish tinge. In quarries among the other slates, of course, you will find much greater variety, and often see a band of quite a different colour running round the rock along the dip of the strata. Compared to such spots, even the finest man-made rock-gardens (as, for instance, the famous White Crags at Clappersgate) look little better than a window-box.

The Borrowdale Volcanic Series

After the Skiddaw Slates had been deposited, a number of volcanoes burst out, probably under the sea, and ejected great masses of lava, ashes and volcanic dust. None of the volcanoes remain, though it is thought that the largest crater may have been near where Bassenthwaite is today, but the material which they poured out formed the rocks known as the Borrowdale Volcanic Series, which make up the central dome of the Lake District. They run side by side with the Skiddaw Slate, roughly parallel with the Penrith–Keswick railway. They then skirt Derwentwater and cross over Honister, missing Buttermere and Crummock and leaving Ennerdale to the granophyre. Next down to Wasdale and along the edge of the Eskdale Granite to the Duddon Estuary. Their south-eastern boundary runs from Broughton-in-Furness, through Coniston and Ambleside and across the Shap fells to the limestone of the Eden Valley. This volcanic area includes nearly all the fells of the centre—the Scafell group, the Coniston-Wetherlam group, the Langdales, Helvellyn and the High Street range. Of the dales it includes Borrowdale, Wasdale, Upper Eskdale, Dunnerdale, Mardale and most of Patterdale. Of the larger lakes only Thirlmere and Haweswater lie entirely in volcanic rock, though Wastwater nearly does. Professor Sedgwick called these rocks "green slates and porphyries". Later geologists have divided them into many groups, some of the names being worth quoting for the joy of the sound: Shap Rhyolite, Shap Andresite, Scafell Ashes and Breccias and the Falcon Crag Group. They vary greatly in hardness since the lavas, ashes and breccias of which they were formed varied greatly in durability, and this has had an immense influence on the scenery. Lava being hard and the ash usually softer, we often get a terraced effect of steep lava cliffs and gentler ash slopes. But where the volcanic ash has been subjected to pressure and squeezed in at the sides it sometimes turns to a slate as hard as iron, and sometimes to a rock that weathers and rots along the lines of the cleavage, breaking away in lumps or dribbling off as small stones. Look at Lord's Rake on Scafell and the western drop of Mickledore above Lingmell Gill at the head of Wastwater—a wall-end that would take blasting and bombing as if they were flea-bites. The ice and the weather have made their marks, and there are long vertical grooves as if the rock had been combed with an iron comb, but still it is harder and more lasting than history.

Where cleavage is greater, however, we find screes or a wreckage of broken-off boulders. The rain oozes into wrinkles of the rock and freezes there, causing a kind of geological rheumatism. The needles of ice swell in the joints of the rock and split it, forming deep cracks and fissures. Then, when the ice melts, the surface of the stone chips and flakes away, and the screes which result are very characteristic of the dales. A scree, by definition, is a slope of loose stones in a state of unstable equilibrium—in other words, if you step on one, it slides. Sometimes the stones are quite large; sometimes, if they are left undisturbed, soil accumulates and grass grows. Sometimes the flood-becks gouge a course through them, washing the rubble to the rivers or lakes to make little gravelly deltas.

The screes which the climber knows, however, are the long cindery slopes which slither under foot—the most magnificent example being at Wasdale. Here, at the lower end of the lake, there is a huge curtain of scree dropping fifteen hundred feet to the water. As they slide downwards the screes grow and gather like streams, till at the foot they splay out in scallops on the lake shore. It is like looking at the fluted columns and fan-vaulting of a cathedral turned upside down.

And there is at least one moment in the year when you can see

them right way up. This is about noon on a clear day in mid-
winter. The sky is cloudless and all the fells north and east of the
lake are blue as speedwell. Down-lake, above Strands, in the throat
of the dale, the sun is skimming through the woods, melting the
hoar-frost and rimming every bough in neon lighting. Even
from the sheep in the fields there rises a fume of luminous steam.
But the sun has not risen above the crest of the screes, and
there is not as yet the least glimmer on the lake itself. It is as if
a solid wedge of shadow had been driven in among the fells.
Then the dark mauve fan-vaulting of the screes re-builds itself
on the water, till it stands on the very floor of the lake, which can
now be seen running out many yards from the shore.

Volcanic rock shows its character no less noticeably when it has
a covering of soil. It is rarely an even covering, for crags and
patches of scree break through in many places. Here there is
grass, here bracken, here (though less of it) heather. Gorse swarms
up the fell-sides and where it seems, unseasonably, to be quite
without flowers it will turn out, as likely as not, to be not gorse
at all but stunted juniper—as, for instance, on the northern flanks
of Wetherlam above Little Langdale. Rowan, thorn, oak and ash
persist quite surprisingly high, in gills and clefts, often padded
between the toes with parsley fern or half drenched in the spray
of a beck. Higher up, above the level of the trees, the vegetation
is still spotted and striped, as if not even the grass could
grow smoothly there. The colour, too, is variegated—brown,
yellow and red among the greens and blues—and everywhere the
rock is poking its fingers out, or crooking a neck round to have
a look at itself. On Harter Fell, a hill above mid-Eskdale, the rock
seems alive, as if it were continually scratching off the scabs of
grass and sedge which accumulate on it.

It is this variegated, shaggy, fussy, bristling texture which gives
to the dales a kind of wholeness. There is no clear division between dale and fell. Stubborn little hay-fields or acres of mangolds
are pegged out high among the crags, while steeples of rock spike
up even from the riverside meadows. The Skiddaw fells stand
rather aloof above the lowlands, but the fells of the dales are one
with the becks and the gills.

The man who goes to the dales goes there for more than scenery.
The views are magnificent when he can get high enough to see
them, but it is not the views that really concern him. It is the feel

and smell of the place, the living company of the dale—the little crags jutting up like gateposts, the redstarts in the bracken, the Herdwicks rubbing themselves against a stile, the farm children throwing stones at an old bucket in the beck.

Yet, if you want views, the volcanic rock can give them. Wasdale is perhaps the most famous, looking up from the lower end of the lake where a shelter has been made by building two walls in the form of a cross:[1] Yewbarrow, on the left; Kirk Fell, half-hidden; Great Gable, plumb in the middle; the lower Lingmell as a foothill to Scafell and Scafell Pike; and the Screes, screening the picture on the right. It is Cumberland's classic landscape, shaped and arranged as by an artist. Indeed, it is shaped almost too perfectly. For the mountains of Wasdale resemble the Forth Bridge in that when you see them for the first time you think, immediately, how like their photographs they are! And you think, a moment later, that the view is not really new to you at all. It is second-hand—a copy of the earlier image you received from book or postcard. It is hard not to be disappointed, not to feel that the landscape is somehow lacking in spontaneity.

So that to see through your own eyes and not through the lens of a camera, you should walk, as it were, out of the picture. Turn your back on the famous view just as you reach its climax, and twist left, along Mosedale Beck between Yewbarrow and Kirkfell. And in about a quarter of a mile you will find yourself on the floor of an enormous wash-tub of a dale, with the broken rim of Pillar and Wind Gap two thousand feet above you. Compared to the emptiness of this scene, Wasdale itself seems as busy as a holiday camp.

Or go to the lake in wet weather, when the clouds split and tear on the pikes like a coat caught on an iron railing and the mist curdles and clears and curdles again along the Screes. The whole dale may be black as tar, or searchlights of sun may strike between the fells, while the wind, roaring up the gap above Nether Wasdale, whips spray off the lake hundreds of feet into the air until it seems to be raining upwards.

[1] The rock exposed on either side of the road along the south-western shore of the lake (i.e. from the foot to about the point where the road from Gosforth joins the road from Wasdale Hall) is, in fact, Ennerdale Granophyre —a sparkling, pinkish rock, rather like Eskdale Granite in general appearance and behaviour.

Of the high fells, Bowfell is rather less exploited by the photo-grapher, though it is surely the most graceful of them all—slender, conical, concave, with an edge to it as if it were gimletting the sky. It is also, of all the central peaks, the one most visible from a distance. Walking through the streets of Millom, you turn a corner, and there, between the gasworks and the Roman Catholic church, is Bowfell.

Perhaps the most famous of all the famous views is that up Derwentwater, from Friar's Crag. Choose to see it, if you can, on a winter day, with snow in the fells, and hoar-frost lying on the dead bracken till the woods seem to be ferny with ostrich feathers. There will be a thin cellophane of ice around the shores, but the centre of the lake will be open. The eye skids across it to Borrow-dale. One crag opens behind another, unfurling like a metal rose, and beyond are Great End and the Scafell Range against the sky. It is not so solemn nor so sculptured as the Wasdale view, but it is richer and more intricate, ravelling the sight in a monkey-puzzle of peaks. It you take the road beside the lake to Grange and Sea-thwaite, you will pass volcanic rock at its most flamboyant. It is almost like a stage show with everything a bit over-sized—an un-tidy tossing-about of rocks and trees, the fat, complacent Bowder Stone, and a waterfall that in wet weather can be seen three or four miles away gushing like a burst reservoir. Castle Crag—the conical, inverted ice-cream-cone of a hill which so delighted the eighteenth-century painters—may even be a block of lava which has cooled in the bottle-neck of an old volcano. In summer this is the most populous of the dales, yet even the hundreds of cars, the coaches and the tents cannot quite diminish its perspective. It remains gothic, grandiose, pinnacled and continually astonishing.

Then, if you swing round on your heels at almost any point on the eastern shore of the lake, there behind you will be Skiddaw, Catbells and the fells of Newlands—the rounded, sulky hum-mocks of the older deposits. There is no more demonstrative contrast between the Skiddaw Slate and the volcanic rock.

The Silurian Rocks

Between the volcanic series and the rocks laid down in the Silurian Period there runs a narrow band of Coniston Limestone which is of much interest to geologists but has very little effect on the appearance of the land. The Silurian rocks, on the

Langdale Pikes (Volcanic Rock)

other hand, make up the third main group of the older rocks of the district and together form most of the southern slopes of the central dome.

They lie almost entirely in North Lancashire and Westmorland, touching Cumberland only in the extreme south. Their northern boundary is the strip of Coniston Limestone lying along the curving edge of the volcanic rocks—Broughton–Coniston–Ambleside–Shap—while in the south they come against the newer limestone around Morecambe Bay, and in the east they meet the Pennines. The area includes Coniston Water, Esthwaite, the dried-up lakes of Kentmere, and all but the most northern tip of Windermere. These rocks were formed like the Skiddaw Slates in a river delta, and are mostly grey in colour, weathering to green or purple, but duller, less sparkling than the volcanic rocks. Near Foxfield, one of the grits has a distinctly reddish tinge, jutting out into the sands of the estuary in a defiant little promontory which only feels the tickle of the sea at the highest point of the tide.

The Silurian rocks are not very assertive. They make up, in the main, the easy-going country south of Coniston and Windermere and between Kendal and Kirby Lonsdale.

The hills here are not very high, and shape themselves often into flattish, rather desolate moorland, dinted with broad, shallow valleys. This not a picture-postcard country, though Coniston, admittedly, has the volcanic range of Dow Crag, Old Man and Wetherlam on one side of the lake, so that John Ruskin, who lived on the other side, said that he looked out on the first great upthrust of mountain Britain.

The contrast is even more memorable when seen from the terminus of the closed-down Foxfield–Coniston branch line. The old platform was vaulted, with a huge arch at the end, through which the Yewdale Crags looked so near that you felt you must be staring through binoculars. They are vicious crags, not very high, but fanged like a tiger, with slaverings of scree and bright green whiskers of larch and birch. Beyond is Raven Crag and the road winding beneath Tom Heights to Ambleside. All this is volcanic. But, from the edge of the platform, you can see Coniston village below you, with the discreet new housing estate and a neat road leading to the lake, beyond which, and behind Ruskin's Brantwood, are the wavy, unemphatic moors of the Silurian Slate.

Park Fell and Elterwater

The Brantwood shore, which looks so dull from the Coniston side, has its own pleasures—woods full of longtailed tits and hawfinches, and little sykes running each through its miniature landscape of rocks, ferns and golden saxifrage. The lake lies north-south, so that, in the early morning, this eastern side is bunched in shadow when the Old Man is already lit from cairn to toe. In the evening, when the water is black with the dazzle, the sun turns a million candle-power on the rowans and alders at the waterside. Brantwood estate has now become a Nature Reserve.

Compared with Coniston, both Windermere and Esthwaite look pretty and harmless, though Esthwaite has its Beatrix Potter woods and Windermere has sickle-like bays and scythe-like reaches which have a late-eighteenth-century romantic grace when seen from the heights of Gummer's How or Moor How. But to sail on Windermere is like going on a child's paddle-boat in a municipal park. There is a promenade at Bowness, with a putting-green nearby; there are hotels and large country houses dug into the wood-slopes like badgers' setts; and, already, motor launches and speed-boats have created a traffic problem on the lake itself. One would not be surprised to learn of *Merrie England* or *Rose Marie* being performed on Belle Isle, with the audience moving backwards and forwards on the ferry.

Windermere was the Victorian bridgehead to the Lakes. It belongs to a time when most visitors came by train and did not move very far. The result, at Bowness, is a sedate, little holiday town which scarcely seems to belong to the fell country at all—an inland watering-place, with neither the elegance of a spa nor the boisterousness of the seaside. Yet there are places only a few miles from Windermere which are even less frequented than the more remote dales. The eastern shore of the lake is given up to the villa and the parked car, but to the west and south there are homely valleys which have little of the self-consciousness and eye-to-business of more celebrated places. There is the Woodland Valley, south of Coniston; the Rusland Valley, south of Windermere; and the valley of the Winster, lying between Windermere and the Kent. Here and there, the land heaves itself into middle-height moorland, neither craggy nor savage, but with saucer-shaped dips and indentations where you can sit alone for hours, even at the height of the holiday season.

The vast, roadless, almost track-less parish of Subberthwaite, between the Crake and the Duddon, has heather up to your waist, marshes green with sphagnum and tarns stuffed with the pink plush of buckbean. Oddly enough, it was one of the more populous parts in prehistoric times. A little further south, above Kirkby-in-Furness, you seem blocked off by the low mounds of the moor from all the familiar sky-lines. Yet a few hundred yards to the east you can look down on the long, slack tentacles of Morecambe Bay, or a few hundred yards to the west, on the Duddon Estuary. This latter view, with all three of the older rocks (Black Combe, the Scafell group and Kirkby Moors) magnificently on show, together with the coastal limestone, the blast furnaces of Millom, the sand, the sea and the Isle of Man, is the most comprehensively Cumbrian view in Cumberland—though, in fact, you are standing in Lancashire.

But for the most part, the Silurian rocks keep well below moor-level, giving a brackeny, bushy, huddled-away, parochial countryside of side-alley valleys and small villages that keep themselves *to* themselves. Many of these belong to the old industrial days of the dales, when power came from the becks and raw material from the woods. There were sawmills, bobbin mills and basket works in many places, and small charcoal-burning blast furnaces at Force Forge in the Rutland Valley, at Nibthwaite, Spark Bridge and Penny Bridge on the Crake (the outlet from Coniston) and at Backbarrow on the Leven (the outlet from Windermere). The Backbarrow furnace, which was opened in the early eighteenth century, went on producing iron until the middle 1960s, and not until 1920 did it change over from charcoal to coke. Nearby are the blue works, the dust from which stains all about it—walls, windows, the road, the hedges, the water in the river and even the ducks.

This industrial origin has given an independence to the villages of the southern valleys. They do not come cap in hand to the visitor. Nor, in fact, does he often go to them, for the simple reason that he does not easily find them. For this is a secretive country, hedged about by woodland. In summer the roads are cluttered and stuffy—the heavy green of chestnut and hazels being held like a golf umbrella over rank bracken and wood-soil alive with ants. There are none of the open glades of the New Forest, but the thick, tight, steaming, anxious, grasping woods of poor soil and a wet climate. So thick is the leafage that in summer you

can walk right past the falls at Force Forge—a fine, wide conglo-
meration of water-slides and swallow dives—and not even notice
that they are there. But in winter the light gets into the woods.
The bracken rots into a dark red thatch, the broom hangs on to
its graveyard green, and the hazel catkins seem to shake out a
yellow pepper of sunlight whenever the wind moves them. The
villages go unconcernedly about their business, shining out,
whitewashed and slaty, among the beckside pastures; Satter-
thwaite, Bouth, Cartmel Fell, Winster, Bowland Bridge, Witherslack. You will scarcely find a picture postcard or an ice-cream
cornet among the lot. But here is a sign of what the Lake District
might still be if the rest of England had not got to know about it.

The Silurian rock has yet one more surprise to offer. In the
south-east there are three small valleys running into the Kent
basin—Kentmere, Longsleddale and Bannisdale. They are all
narrow and tucked away—less rhetorical than the central dales,
though the first two of them look up to exhilarating dale-heads
among the older rocks above Mardale. Kentmere and Longsleddale are well lived-in and easy to reach, yet each is unexploited,
unspoiled without being "preserved" as a museum piece. Kentmere, indeed, has for its protection the workings of a large deposit of
diatomaceous earth used in the making of heat insulated bricks
among other things. The main buildings, though not very prepossessing, are fairly well screened by trees, while the diggings and
the little aerial rope-way have a Heath Robinson charm which in
no way harms the dale. Longsleddale is a farming valley, with
straight, steep, level walls of fell on either side. After heavy rain
the water pours down gill after gill till the dale looks like a street
of terraced houses with the roof gutters all burst.

Longsleddale and Kentmere have been saved from the traffic and
summer turmoil of, say, Little Langdale by the fact that they have
no through road. A track from Kentmere leads over Nan Bield
Pass to the head of Haweswater, and one from Longsleddale over
Gatescarth to the same spot, and both were once important
trans-Lakes routes. But the motorist, having reached Kentmere
Church or Sadgill has to turn round and go back, and so long as
he has to do so, that part of the district will be able to hold on to
much of its native character.

In Bannisdale he is unlikely even to turn round since, there is
no surfaced road at all beyond the bottom-end of the valley, and

if he persists in going further, he may have to do as I did, and get a farm tractor to drag his car out of the mud. You approach from the Shap road over a stretch of upland, so that when you come down to the beck again near Dryhowe Farm you seem to be entering not a valley but a trough, closed at both ends. In some ways it looks as if it might belong to the Pennines rather than the Lakes, for its shape is that of the modelled dint and roll of a Yorkshire dale rather than that of the chiselled groove of a Lake valley. The rain pours into it as into a bucket and there seems no need to dam it to hold the water there.

But that is precisely what Manchester Corporation wished to do, though the scheme has been dropped, at least temporarily, along with the plan to draw water from Ullswater. The Planning Board of the Lake District National Park protested, of course, and so did the Friends of the Lake District, but there was no great public outcry to save Bannisdale. It does not have its thousands of visitors, like Ullswater, and it has not been the shelter of a village community as Mardale has been—there are, in fact, only two farms in the whole dale. Yet those of us who think of the Lakes as a living entity, rooted in the rock and in the lives of past generations, could not let this spot go without regret, for perhaps nowhere else has retained so much of the bare, starve-acre, locked-off-from-the-world character of the dales that Wordsworth knew. To drown Bannisdale would be to drown history.

Eskdale Granite

Long after the central rocks had been formed a number of igneous rocks were thrust up among them, probably in the period known as Old Red Sandstone. The main masses are the granite of Shap, Skiddaw and Eskdale, the granophyre of Ennerdale, the micro-granite of Threlkeld and the general mix-up of rocks on Carrock Fell. There are also many dykes and minor intrusions including a patch of the rare minette on Sale Fell near Bassen-thwaite.

The best known commercially of the granites are those of Shap and Threlkeld, both of which are quarried for road material and for making kerbs and setts for pavements. Shap granite will take a high polish, when it looks like frozen potted meat and is used as an ornamental stone. But the Eskdale granite is much more extensive than either of these and has a far greater effect on the landscape.

At first glance this effect is not obvious. It is true that when the river burrows its way like a woodworm out of the heart of Upper Eskdale it finds itself in the less austere mid-reaches of the valley. At Doctor's Bridge, near The Woolpack Inn, it scurries through upland meadows of cow-wheat, betony, wood vetch and the greater burnet which gives the best of all the home-made wines. There are inns, a guest-house or two, the Outward Bound School, and the old, lost-away church of St. Catherine's, half islanded by the river. But below Eskdale Green the dale is almost empty again, the main road having turned off into Miterdale. A minor road, however, runs from near the house where the Eskdale and Ennerdale Foxhounds are kennelled to Muncaster Bridge on the Whitehaven–Millom route, and all along this road you are in what seems like a typical Cumberland dale. There are the steep, craggy sides. There is the almost-flat bottom, with the river winding among shingle, willows and willowherb, until it meets the herons and yellow flags of the sea marshes long before it gets any sight of the sea. But if you have an eye for rock you soon begin to notice that there is something odd about it. It is the wrong colour to begin with, and has an unusual glint. The walls are piled together just like ordinary walls in the fells, but the stones are not slate but chunks of granite. It is as if the architect of the Lake District, continuing to work to his original plan, had finished off Eskdale in imported material.

Eskdale Granite varies a good deal in colour, being sometimes a mercury-like grey with only a hint of pink, and sometimes the dark red of iron ore which has, in fact, been mined in the dale. Stone of this kind was used for the older buildings of many of the railway stations between Millom and Whitehaven. It is so dark and red that it looks almost like red sandstone, and, as the window-sills and kerbs and many of the platform walls *are* of sandstone, it is easy to confuse the two. You can distinguish between them, however, even from a passing train, by noticing the way the stones are laid. The freestone is shaped into rectangles and laid horizontally like bricks; the granite is jigsawed together in pieces of uneven size and shape, with the pattern of the joins picked out by mortar.

Perhaps the easiest way to inspect this rock is by taking a trip on the Eskdale Miniature Railway, the "Ratty Railway", which has a gauge of fifteen inches and was laid down in the 1870s to carry ore from the mines at Boot. Later it provided transport for the people of Eskdale and Irton and, after 1922, carried granite from the quarries as well as being an extra attraction for visitors. As local transport it has been entirely superseded by cars and buses, and in the later 1950s it seemed more and more likely that it would have to close down. In 1961, however, it was taken over by a railway preservation society, and since then has carried a record number of passengers. All South Cumbrians hope that it may survive a little longer, if only as a sentimental anachronism.

To children and train-spotters, it seems more up-to-date than the ordinary railways. The engines, for instance, are not toys but powerful Shetland ponies of machinery which can face the steepish climb up the dale. The carriages are open[1] like cattle-trucks and you sit, two by two, facing one another, and knocking your knees together as the train bounces down on the return journey.

The line begins not in Eskdale but in Miterdale, the small valley which lies between Eskdale and Wasdale. The sea at this point makes a three-pronged flank attack on the fells, and nowhere else on Cumberland coast does it probe so far inland. At Ravenglass, where the three prongs (the Esk, the Mite, and the Irt) are joined on to the main shaft of the estuary, you will see scurvy grass and sea-plaintain growing beside the heather, and the fishing-boats are drawn up as if the foot-hills were docks. The railway runs beside the salt marshes of the Mite and then climbs the slopes of Muncaster Fell. This is real granite country. It is on a small scale, like the railway, but everywhere there are chippings and crusts of rock which sparkle in the turf. The children cheer as the train runs under bridges or across becks. They lean over the edge of the trucks till you feel sure they will fall out. They snatch at ferns and the white frilly flowers of keck or cow-parsley, and if they are careless enough to snatch at the bracken they are likely to get their hands slashed by the sharp stalks. The train slows down in places, chugging up the inclines, and the rowans bend over it, almost knocking the chimney off the engine. There are

[1] Covered carriages were introduced in 1962.

wild roses and golden rod among the fern, so that if you like to take a risk you can jump out, grab a handful, and jump back into the train again. At one place the line passes near the quarries and you can see artificial screes of the pink rock and the whitish-pink dust from the crushing machine. At Eskdale Green it finds a dip in the hill and enters Eskdale proper at a spot close to the route of the Roman road from Ambleside. It arrives, as it were, by the tradesman's entrance, behind the walls and hedges of back gardens, and hustles to the terminus at Dalegarth. The children get out, many of them being met by their parents who have driven up from Ravenglass by car. The Victorian visitors went without fail to see the waterfall in the deep, unkempt chasm of Stanley Gill, romantic as an old wood-engraving. Present-day visitors, educated by television, are more likely to go to see the Roman fort at Hardknott.

The Newer Rocks: Mountain Limestone

After the older rocks of the Lake District had been laid down and humped into a dome, the becks and the rivers began to carve out the valleys, which, from the beginning, probably took the same general direction as those of today. Then the land sank, there was a semi-tropical climate, and the carboniferous rocks were deposited. Up came the land again, and the new rock was peeled off until the older rock was exposed once more. There was another sinking and the Permian rocks were laid down at a time when desert extended over much of what we now call Europe. Another elevation and these latest rocks were stripped away, perhaps 30,000 feet of them, but round the main dome of the Lake District some still remain like the rings round Saturn. The oldest of these newer rocks, and that which makes up the innermost ring, is the Carboniferous or Mountain Limestone, which also forms much of the Pennine Chain. This has been called the backbone of England, and rightly so for it really is bone, the bone or skeletal remains of millions of sea-creatures.

The limestone ring round the Lake District is broken and irregular but only along the Cumberland coast is it completely missing. Let us start at the north-western tip and follow it clockwise. It appears near Beckermet, and runs thence along the line of the mining towns of Egremont, Cleator Moor, and Frizington to Cockermouth. This is only a narrow strip but it has been of great importance to West Cumberland since here the rock contains iron ore. Beyond Cockermouth the limestone curves round the back of Skiddaw through Caldbeck to Penrith where it meets the sandstone of the Eden Valley. From thence it continues in a wide belt, keeping just north of Ullswater and Haweswater, until it reaches the Yorkshire border, where the Pennines themselves stand as a tangent to the circle. The southern segment is more broken. There is a large patch round Arnside which pushes up the lower Kent as far as Kendal. There are a few smaller patches round Grange-over-Sands and Cartmel; and from Ulverston on Morecambe Bay to Askam on the Duddon the rock is all limestone, except around Barrow. Across the Duddon it appears again at Hodbarrow and Kirksanton. The Furness and South Cumberland deposits are small but, like those of Egremont, they are rich —or once were rich—in iron ore.

The mountain limestone is one of the loveliest rocks to be found in the whole district, and forms a soft, white ruff round the head of the slates. Not that it is always soft. The Pennines are not soft and descend westward in magnificent escarpments into the Eden Valley from Brough to Appleby. Nor is the fell country round Askham and Bampton in any way soft, though it is not magnificent either. It is bare, but not with the clean-cut bareness of Skiddaw Slate. Instead, it seems a landscape of utter poverty—as if a flock of monstrous, prehistoric fowls had scratched and scratched till the rock were scored and scurfy.

The best-known part of the limestone country, however, is that around the shores of Morecambe Bay where the rock is much gentler and more agreeable. Most visitors to the Lakes pass through this limestone area, entering it round about Carnforth. And, immediately, they must notice a difference in the *feel* of the land. It is still quite an ordinary type of landscape, quiet, grassy and green, though beautifully clean and washed after the grime of central Lancashire. The little chips which break through the soil here and there are as white as daisies. The stone walls, the cottages, the farms look as if they had been scrubbed.

North of Carnforth the country is colder and bonier, and the rock begins to show its teeth in the hills which divide the River Kent from the River Gilpin. On the Gilpin side the land drops in the long Underbarrow Scar—a chalky, scree-like escarpment that looms, white or ochre, above the mists of the river marshes.

On the Kendal side it descends in alternate shelves of white rock and terraces of green turf. Here and there, throughout this area, and again around Cartmel and Ulverston, the hills seem from a distance to have been dusted with lime, but when you get close you find that they are covered with crusts and cobbles of rock like tippings of slag. Sometimes the water seeps below the surface, dissolving the rock and hollowing it out until you walk on a shell of stone. In many of the little hills around the River Bela, and again near Arnside and Silverdale, there are waves and crests of rock, with crevasses more than leg-deep, and small white scrapings of scree. Near Beetham are the Fairy Steps—a narrow, half-natural staircase ascending a fissure in the rock. My grandmother was born nearby, and when, years later, tapping the floor with her crutch, she told me that she used to watch the fairies running up and down the steps it did not occur to me to doubt her.

On Arnside Knott and in the easy uplands behind Arnside Tower the limestone loses its poverty-stricken look. Here the land is bushy and, on the Silverdale side, the trees walk right down into the sea. There are thick, dark woods, in some places so tightly thatched with hazel and the smaller trees that you have to creep to enter them. In parts, too, they seem almost soil-less—the roots of the trees gripping bare ribs and ledges of rock. These are the woods of the wild lily-of-the-valley and the rarer Herb Paris—though the lily is likely to become just as rare if people continue to dig it up. Outside, in the sunshine, are the limestone flowers—gentians, rock-roses, cowslips and the tall yellow turrets of Ploughman's Spikenard. (Until recently the latter flower had not been recorded in Cumberland, but a year or two ago I found it well established at the extreme southern tip of the county on the limestone rocks of Hodbarrow. I like to think that my grandmother, who came to Hodbarrow from Beetham in 1867, may have brought the seeds in her boots.)

From Silverdale right round to Roa Island on the extreme north-west horn of Morecambe Bay the rock of the shore-line is mostly limestone. Around the Kent Estuary, in particular, there are limestone cliffs dropping sheer into—not the sea, but flat, drained marshes, with straight ditches and canals and long embankments to hold back the tide.

All along the shore by Grange-over-Sands, and again in Low

Furness, from Bardsea to Aldingham, the rock comes down to the sea in gentle shelvings. Here the water laps the stone like a cat licking butter, smoothing and rounding it till it takes the shapes of the organic world—of beech boughs and fungi, of rhubarb leaves, roots and tubers. Billows and ripples are left moulded into the rock, crested as if they were about to break, and pebbles have been trapped in hollows, scooping out pot-holes. Sometimes the shore seems crowded with bathers, all carved from stone by Henry Moore. In the sockets and navels of the rock thrift grows, pink and papery, and in one or two places the rarest flower in Lancashire, the bloodless Bloody Cranesbill of Walney Island, has gained a root-hold on the mainland.

So far limestone may have seemed to be more of a neighbour to the Lakes than a part of them. But in some of the valleys which run down to Morecambe Bay it walks right in among the hills of the slate. The lower valley of the River Winster is the most memorable. Here, on your left as you go up, you have the dark, blue-khaki slates of Newton Fell and Cartmel Fell—open, undemonstrative moorland above and scrubby, beck-ridden woods below; and, on your right, the white land-slide of Whitbarrow Scar. Travelling north along the main road you are aware of much the same contrast. From Levens Bridge to Gilpin Bridge you are facing White Scar—an enormous chunk of crumbling Lancashire cheese. You pass the Witherslack road-end and climb the hill of Lindale, and from thence to Newby Bridge[1] you are running beside a spirited rough-and-tumble of Silurian slate, the last main outcrop of this rock to the south.

In Furness, beyond Ulverston, there is not so much rock on the surface, but you are never allowed to forget that you are in limestone country because of the whiteness of the buildings. Even the ruins—and there are many in the mining districts—have the same whiteness. Most of the ruins of Cumberland and Westmorland are of melancholy sandstone or of slate; but the limestone ruins are sprightly and youthful. The farms on the fell-side shine out as if they had been white-washed, while many of the villages have a smug prettiness which in other parts of England would fill them with cocktail bars and photographers. Here they are

[1] To avoid confusion it may be mentioned that Levens Bridge crosses the River Kent, while Newby Bridge crosses the River Leven just below the point where it flows out of Windermere.

just left alone. The country between the Ulverston–Barrow road
and the Aldingham shore is a Lancashire Cotswolds, without
the architectural harmony of that area but with all its haphazard,
rambler-rose-and-pigstye felicity.

There are many quarries up and down the limestone areas—
some of them huge, deserted craters, full to the brim with water,
and hung with willows and ferns; others, raw wounds with the
broken bones sticking out and a fug of powdery scurf all about
them. Between Dalton-in-Furness and Askam-in-Furness the
quarrymen have blasted away half a hillside, while at Silverdale
they have given acres of woodland a perpetual winter of chalky
frost. Limestone is one of the most valuable of all the Lake rocks,
being used, among other things, to help to smelt the iron ore
which it contains.

New Red Sandstone

The coal measures touch only the extreme edge of our area,
but the Penrith and St. Bees Sandstones make a rather more conspicuous mark on the Lake scene, forming the second or outer
ring of the newer rocks—though what is left is actually the shape
of a horseshoe hanging upside down so that the luck falls out.

Beginning, then, with the left-hand point of the horseshoe, the
sandstone emerges in the lower end of Furness around Barrow,
and runs up the Cumberland coast to Whitehaven where it is
interrupted by the coal measures. It re-emerges at Maryport, and
thence covers much of the Cumberland Plain as far as Carlisle,
while the right limb of the horseshoe is thrust down almost the
whole length of the Eden Valley, past Penrith and Appleby to the
Yorkshire border. Most of the sandstone, therefore, lies outside
the Lake area, and even where it comes into that area it does not
often bring itself to your notice. You can walk along the Cumberland coast, from Haverigg in the south as far as Seascale, and not
once suspect that you are in sandstone country. Even the farms
are built either of slate from the hills or of cobble-ducks gathered
on the shore and glued together with mortar. At Seascale, however, when the tide is out, you see a paving of low, dark rocks,
mildewed with seaweed, while at Netherton, a few miles further
north, the rock suddenly bites. Here there is a superb red beach—
slabs of stone broken and flaked like ruined steps going down to
the sea. At St. Bees there is a small graceful curve of shingle—

now unnecessarily smarmed into a little promenade—and then the south headland of Tomlin. This is a huge hull of rock, blunt-edged, rough as emery-paper, shoving its rusty steel-plating straight into the sea. Beyond Tomlin there is the little, secret Fleswick Beach, and then the cliffs thrust out again before curving in to the harbour at Whitehaven.

This double-headland of St. Bees is the finest stretch of coastal scenery between Scotland and Wales—the only spot, many visitors may think, where the Cumberland coast lives up to what they had expected. Away from the shore the sandstone very rarely obtrudes, except in the small chasms gouged out by the river around Calder Abbey. Here the rock pushes through the green of the turf, or flakes and splits away into small terraces among the trunks of the trees, where the dead leaves pile up. Green and red are the colours here—not the green and red of holly leaf and berry, but a dark, sluggish green and a sombre brown-red which merge in the trodden mud of autumn. The Calder, indeed, though it has nothing of the scope and ceremony of Cumberland's other sandstone river, the Eden, is different from anything else in the Lakes. Most of the Lake rivers, for all their individuality, are a set of variations on two or three themes. Calder has a theme to itself. It is, largely, a theme unheard, for above the Abbey, this is one of the least visited of rivers. You follow it, walking along the edge of steep, sandstone banks, dark and top-heavy with rhododendrons. At Thornholme the road is no more than a cart track beneath the lumpy moorland, and the river ploughs deeply into clay and rock, scooping a course fifty feet below field level. It is hard to believe that you are only a few miles from Wasdale or Ennerdale for this scene might belong to the Pennines or the country of the Roman Wall—say, the gorge of the Irthing below Birdoswald. But when you climb back to the moor, there in the dip of the valley, you see the cooling towers of the atomic power station at Calder Hall, and for the next few minutes there will be no need to remind you where you are.

The mark of the sandstone is not entirely confined to St. Bees and the Calder, even in West Cumberland. For sandstone quarries have provided much of the building material along the coast, especially for churches, old and new. The two main abbeys of the Lakes, Calder and Furness, both lie in sandstone glades. (Shap, the only abbey of Westmorland, lies in the limestone of the

Lowther Valley, and, to Cumbrian eyes, looks the wrong colour for religion.) In the older churches (St. Bees Priory, or Isel, or Waberthwaite) the sober, ecclesiastic stone weathers green and dank as an old bowler hat. In those of more recent date (St. George's, Millom, or on the new top to the tower of St. Bees) it remains rosy and warm. The stone is much used in some of the villages near St. Bees—Seascale, Beckermet and Gosforth, in particular—so that the approach to Wasdale from the west is past cottages, mansions, churches and schools that are solid, square, dark red and stubbornly unpicturesque.

Many of the atomic scientists from Windscale and Calder Hall now live in these villages, and it seems grimly appropriate that the rock formed in the deserts of the past should house the men who are likely to turn the future into another desert.

III

THE SHAPING OF THE ROCKS

The Coming of the Ice

IT has been said that when God made England His finger touched but did not press, but that is not true of Cumberland and Westmorland. He pressed there all right. What is more, He used His nails. And the nails were ice.

If the ice had not come the general shape of the country, the cartwheel of dales and ridges, might be much the same as it is now, but the features would have been very different. There would have been few cliffs or crags, no waterfalls, no gills, and perhaps no lakes. The ice invaded the North of England from two main directions. From Scandinavia it came to the north-east coast, covering much of Durham and Yorkshire, but rarely crossing beyond the Pennines; from Scotland it came down the west coast, covering the Carlisle Plain and filling the sea-basin between there and the Isle of Man. This Scottish ice carved deeply into the spurs of the western fells, which once sloped gently to the sea, but now drop steeply to the two-or-three-mile-wide coastal plain. It pushed arms of ice up the estuaries. It broke chunks off the Eskdale Granite and left them deposited on Walney Island and further south. It blocked the mouths of some of the western valleys, forming lakes such as the "Whicham Lake" beneath Black Combe, which must have been rather like the Bassenthwaite of today.

The main glaciation, however, was home produced. As the mean temperature fell and more and more snow accumulated every year a glacier began to form in each dale, until eventually the lower hills were submerged and only the higher central peaks stood like an archipelago above the slow tides of ice. Perhaps even these went under in the end. The reverse must have been the case when the ice retreated. First it ebbed from the central dome, then left bare the radiating ridges, and finally oozed out of each separate dale. As the coastal glaciers, the Scottish Ice, shrank back, step by step, from the south, the waters burst out of the valleys.

47

That is how Walney Island was formed—the water in what is now the Duddon Estuary escaping round the southern end of the glacier to gouge out Walney Channel. This coming and going of the ice took place several times, with periods of comparatively temperate climate in between. But details of this sort, though they are of great importance to the geologist, matter little to one whose main concern is with the general look and lie of the land. What matters to him is that when the ice had gone it left a changed country.

Glacial Deposits

The deposits are the least interesting of the effects of glaciation. There are daubs of boulder-clay or gravels at many places along coast—dull, humpy moraines, kettle-holed with ponds, half-choked with sedges, water-pepper, fool's-celery, bur-reed and all the smelly, green-flowered weeds of stagnant water. Among the fells, the glacial drift dammed up side-valleys or combes, so giving rise to the tarns or even, in the case of Ennerdale, to one of the larger lakes.

More engaging than the moraines, however, are the erratic boulders carried by the ice and left perched in odd places, often on the top of a small hill. The Bowder Stone in Borrowdale is the most famous of them as well as being by far the biggest, though it is so handy that it is hard not to feel that it was put there as a side-show for visitors. There are lots of smaller examples, especially along the coast, most of them looking cheerfully ridiculous—huge Humpty Dumpties of rock, stranded at the back of a housing estate for cows to rub against or boys to use as a shelter for a camp fire. Many were left, in the first place, insecurely balanced on the fell-side whence they rolled down to the bottom of the valley—which is one of the reasons why such rivers as the Derwent are chock-full of stones in parts of their course.

Valleys

But far more interesting than the glacial deposits are the effects of glacial erosion.

Let us look first at what the ice did to the shape of a valley. A cross-section of a normal—i.e. an un-glaciated—valley would be V-shaped, the sides sloping evenly from top to bottom. When the ice got to work, however, it sliced off the sides till they were

Granite boulders—River Esk

nearly perpendicular, and broadened and planed the valley floor, so that a cross-section would now be U-shaped. In the Lake District we have dales with steep, bare sides, below which a flat strip of fertile land runs right up into the heart of the mountains. From the upland slopes, they appear as green corridors lying below the brown, grey, purple and blue of the fell-sides.

When the ice carved away the sides of the valleys it left what had been smaller tributary valleys hanging in the air like an upstairs landing in a half-demolished house, leading to nowhere. Such broken-off valleys give us some of the loneliest spots among the fells—a desolation of stones and bracken, walled off by massive cliffs of silence. The becks, as if still surprised not to be taking their pre-Ice-Age course, plunge to the valley-bed, and if the rock of the cliff-face is particularly hard, or if the rock on which the water drops is particularly soft, then we have one of the typical Lake District waterfalls[1]—a thin stream of water falling uninterruptedly for sixty feet or more, or perhaps taking the drop in two consecutive leaps.

The Victorians loved waterfalls. Waterfalls were so obviously ornamental, so tasteful, so discreet and damp and crepuscular—the kind of small-scale, fanciful landscape they would have constructed for themselves had they been God. The paths to the falls were well marked out, with plank bridges and handrails, so that you could cross and re-cross the beck, drawing closer and closer until at last you stood with the drizzle of the spray on your face. At some of the the more popular falls, such as Dalegarth Force in Eskdale, the farmer posted an old woman at the gate to collect sixpences as if he were the one to thank for turning on the tap to start the performance.

But waterfalls are not greatly in fashion today. The more famous and accessible are still visited—Aira Force, Scale Force and so on. But the path to Colwith Force is scarcely trodden, while at Dalegarth the beck is so overgrown that you can hardly push near enough to see the falls at all. Now I share the taste of the Victorians, but, alas, I do not share their legs and wind and cannot scramble up a rough gill to see many of the falls I would like to see. I am grateful, therefore, to those which do not hide themselves away: to Dungeon Gill, which after rain, can be seen from the

[1] They may also be caused by the deflection of the beck from its original course, and may coincide with faults in the rock.

Limestone clints near Cockermouth

valley-bottom sprouting out of the fellside. I am grateful, too, to
the falls along the glaciated flanks of Black Combe—falls so little
famed that they have not even names. In dry weather they have
not much water either. But in wet weather the drainage of mile
upon mile of upland pours over the edge of the western escarpment as copiously as if someone were swilling the fells down.
When the becks are frozen in winter they hang down the black
sides of the rock like rags of lace.

Gills

More often, however, the beck from a hanging valley cuts out
a gill, and descends not in one or two leaps but in a jingling chain
of hops and hoops. One of the best known is at Tilberthwaite,
where you can ascend half a mile or more of rickety bridges,
many of them, unfortunately, now rotting away. When you
remember how short a time, geologically speaking, the water
has had to work on the rock—the shortest estimate puts the final
retreat of the ice at about 10,000 years ago—you realize the great
erosive power of even small streams.

I remember with affection a gill on the Brantwood side of
Coniston Water. It was September and the woods were full of
blackberries, tutsan and browning fern. I had a farm dog with me,
a young bitch who was afraid of water—rather oddly so, since all
the rest of the farm dogs enjoyed swimming in the lake. The dog
went ahead, out of sight, and eventually I found that it had turned
into a little cleft and had run round the edge of the rock basin
and could not find its way back. After spending about ten minutes
trying to show it how to circumnavigate the pool, or, alternative-
ly, to persuade it to venture into the water, I gave up and left.
Ten seconds later the dog rejoined me, having solved its own
problem in a dash of despair.

This rock basin or grotto had been formed by quite a small
beck or syke falling over a cliff almost twelve feet high. The sides
sloped very steeply, of smooth Silurian slate, and in the bottom
was a pool, green, still and clear. Down went the sides until they
met at a sharp angle well below the surface of the water. Directly
opposite the fall the cliffs dropped to a kind of conduit where the
water ran out and I had come in. A few feet lower down it was
once again an ordinary, unpretentious, little stream, bubbling
and wriggling over stones and the mossy roots of hazels.

Dunnerdale

There is no better example of a lakeless dale than Dunnerdale. It is narrow, compact, self-contained, and does not dwindle away at its foot, as does Langdale, nor splay out like the lake valleys of Wasdale and Borrowdale. Wordsworth, in his Duddon Sonnets, followed the river from its source to the sea, but it is better to track it in the opposite direction.

At Duddon Bridge you have the salt marshes of the estuary just below you, and the "jaws" of the dale ahead—High Duddon, muffled in rhododendrons, on the Cumberland side of the river, and Bank End on the Lancashire side. The main road climbs up Bank End so that you enter the dale, as it were, from above. On either side are steep scars of woodland, swilled with green in spring, and in autumn as fiery and challenging as a red-haired girl. Down in the valley bottom the river seeps off under cover of hazels among banks of·shingle, wild garlic and daffodils. It is a flittering, twittering, rippling, restless, hunting, dodging, never-still world of longtailed tits, dippers, water-rats, weasels and otters. It is also a world of ants—millions upon millions of them, turning all the leaf-mould into one huge ant-hill and even covering the branches of the trees like flies.

But up on the main road you are already on the open moor. The walls have been got rid of, and the Lancashire side of the dale is steep and rough, with black junipers among the screes, and the old, unused pack-horse road to Broughton Mills cobbled like a causeway up the crack of a dried-up gill. Dunnerdale is probably the best of all the dales to visit in late autumn or winter, for it faces due south, so that the low, midday sun pours straight into it. If you are facing updale there is not a shadow to be seen: the bracken is on fire up miles of fell-side. The dead birch leaves, the little conifer shapes of the mosses, the chips of quartz in the rock, all gleam in every detail as if they were on show in a jeweller's window.

At Ulpha Bridge the river is confined for a few yards between narrow rocks. It is very deep here, and green as bile, but below the church it widens out, and someone has planted a row of conifers, well-spaced and elegant. For the first mile and a half above Ulpha the scene is surprisingly docile, and the valley-bottom is as tidy as a strip of Cheshire. Then the road leaves the river and wanders off to meet the big beck which bounces down from

Seathwaite Tarn. "Wonderful Walker's" church stands in Seathwaite and some distance above this, forty years ago, I first saw
the signpost pointing simply to

THE LANGDALES.

In fact, it points to a fracas of rock and rowan and rough pasture
through which the road winds like a sheep-trod across a scree.

This is the point where a track swings to the right into the one
substantial tributary valley of Dunnerdale, and then curves past
Holling House, out on to the open fell and over Walna Scar. And
it is from the lower slopes of this pass—a kind of side-entrance
into Dunnerdale—that you can get the finest vantage point for
viewing the dale as a whole. Below you is the small, tureen-shaped
valley of Tarn Beck, divided from the main dale by a low hump.
Upwards, the valley pushes past the hirsute cone of Harter
Fell to the three-fold camel-humps of Scafell, Scafell Pike and
Great End, which look as if they belong to the head of the Duddon
instead of to Eskdale and Wasdale. Downwards, the dip of the
river takes a long left turn beneath silver, civilized woods, until
the heave of Hesk Fell and the back of Black Combe block
out the rest of the view.

Turning updale at the "Langdale" signpost we soon find our-
selves back beside the Duddon which had been hidden from us
in the cleft of the Duddon Gorge where it batters its way through
rolled and tumbled boulders. This is the romantic country of mid-
Dunnerdale, bright as a border ballad, prickly with larches and
brindled with heather and rowan berries, where the river is
in a continual jingle of what Wordsworth called "would-be
water-falls".

At Birk's Bridge there is another chasm—the narrowest and
deepest in the dale—and the river runs under a tunnel of oaks
and alders, beneath which the leg-rock sits perpetually soaking
its corns. Then the country changes and the dale-head opens out,
hollow and bare, and soon we come to the old ruined farm of
Hinning House (from the Middle English "Haining"— an enclosure), with close beside it the new houses built by the Forestry
Commission and appropriately screened by trees.

For yet another quarter of a mile or so the dale-bottom is
as flat as the seashore, and the river runs among hay-fields and

glacial gravel. This is the combe or corric, the rounded dale-head, very characteristic of glaciated valleys, where the top-end of the glacier has bitten back deeply into the rock. Then, at Cockley Beck, the dale is really over and the river swings to the right, towards Wrynose Pass, and splits up into many small becks any one of which may claim to be the source of the Duddon. Thirty years ago, when the track was still un-metalled, I pushed a bicycle over Wrynose. All the way up I promised myself a view from the top and a free-wheel down the other side into Little Langdale. There was no free-wheel, however, because the surface was like a stone wall pushed over. And, to begin with, there was not much view—only sour bog, with shrunken dubs and pools such as you can find at sea-level behind the dunes. It was, I felt, rather an anti-climax. But, there, at the side of the track, was the Three Shires Stone, marking the end of Cumberland and the end of Dunnerdale, and two minutes later I was looking down into a new county.

Lakes

The ice not only carved the sides of a valley but also planed its floor, and in doing so it worked in fits and starts according to the hardness of the rock, so that the incline from source to sea is not even but variable, and the river at times flows quietly through flattish meadows and at times tumbles down a steep slope.

Frequently, too, the ice gouged deeply into the rock floor and slid up again, scooping out a hollow well below the general level of the dale-bottom, and here, when the ice melted, a lake would form, with its shores often heightened by glacial débris.

Sometimes, instead of grinding away the surface of the rock, the ice "plucked" at it, along the line of the cleavage, and when this happened we find that the whole bed of a river falls perpendicularly, giving us the kind of waterfall of which Skelwith Force is typical. Here the waters of the Brathay, which have been sliding along from Elterwater, suddenly drop twenty or thirty feet. Because of the weight of the water and because it drops, as it were, "solid", such falls are often more impressive than many which are far higher. The water gains speed as it approaches the force, and then twists in mid-air as it falls, and in spite of the turmoil the effect is one of steadiness. We seem to be looking at a sculpture in glass. The light dithers and sparkles on the surface and bubbles skitter continually among the rocks, but the fall itself is constant and still.

The Changing Scene

Because of the immense ages of time which have gone towards the shaping of the landscape as we see it today we are inclined to think that change belongs to the past. We speak of "The Unchanging Hills" and think of the apparent permanence of nature as distinct from the transitoriness of man. But—except for the glaciers—the forces of change are still at work today—frost, rain, wind, sun and rivers. The landscape is not dead nor static, a mere relic of the past: it is a living thing, at every moment changing and developing before our eyes.

Perhaps the most obvious changes are those taking place in the lakes and tarns, all of which are steadily silting up. Scores, perhaps hundreds, of tarns have already been filled and are now peat bogs on the fell-side. In Kentmere a whole lake has disappeared, the process having been helped on by drainage. At the head of practically all the lakes which still remain there is a large stretch of flat land formed out of the mud washed down by the main river of the upper dale. Haweswater is an exception merely because here the water-level has been artificially raised. At Coniston, two considerable streams flow into the head of the lake—Yewdale Beck from Tilberthwaite and Church Beck from the Old Man. Both of these pass near old quarries or mine workings, so that both have brought down immense amounts of rubble, soil and quarry-dust, until they have built up acres of stony delta between the village and the jetty from which the Lake steamer used to sail. Parts of the water edge are so deep in ooze and so thick with ten-foot reeds that you can push a boat into them and find yourself completely caged in a jungle of brown and green blades. If the process continues, then we may find that the top end of the lake, opposite Tent Lodge, may be detached from the rest and become a small tarn like the Priest Pot, above Esthwaite Water.

Sometimes, too, a large and powerful beck enters a lake half-way down its course. Then, if there is no strong current, the delta which forms is likely, in the end, to cut the lake in two. Such multiplication by fission has already taken place in the case of Buttermere and Crummock and also in that of Derwentwater and

Bassenthwaite, both pairs of lakes being more or less re-united in times of flood. In the second example, the intervening delta is now just as big as either of the remaining lakes, since the original Derwent-Bassenthwaite-water was assailed on either flank by a stream of considerable carrying power—Newlands Beck on the west and the Greta on the east.

A somewhat similar silting-up is going on in the coastal estuaries. Ravenglass was an important harbour in the times of the Romans and continued to receive small trading vessels right up to the middle of the nineteenth century, but today it stands on an almost land-locked creek. Along the edges of most of the river-mouths, especially those around Morecambe Bay, dykes and embankments have helped to drain the salt marshes and bring good land to the farmer. Much more could be done and perhaps some of the estuaries could be reclaimed entirely.

Such marshland farming, however, is common to the larger estuaries of all the English coasts, and it is only above the line of the salt that the silting has taken on a true Lake character. For here vast acres of peat or mosses have accumulated in valley-bottoms that were once visited by the high tides. Few people realize how far inland these peat bogs penetrate. Along Kirkby Pool from the Duddon, beside Holker Hall in Cartmel, and landwards of Levens Bridge along the River Gilpin and Underbarrow Pool, they push right up among the hills. The Old Rectory at Woodland, in the valley of Kirkby Pool, stands, fifteen miles from the coast, on a rocky knoll, with a tumble of crags around it and some of the wildest, most Highland-looking country in all the Lakes. Yet it is only fifty feet above sea-level, and a little lower down the valley there are miles of peat moss, crossed only by cart tracks, over the boot-tops in mud. The drains are dug ten feet deep and the becks run far below the level of the ground. It is a country which is always brown, for the spring does not seem to draw up enough new green rushes to blot out the dead ones of last year. There are copses and hedges-run-wild of birches and willows, and bankings that look like burial mounds. It is a land of plovers and shelducks, belonging to the England of before the Enclosure Act. You might be in John Clare's Northamptonshire or in parts of the New Forest of today. Yet when you raise your eyes above the willow-line, you see the unmistakably Cumbrian bull-neck of Black Combe. My grandmother grew up beside the River Bela between Milnthorpe

and Arnside. At night, as a girl, she would gaze across the blackness of the sands or the blackness of the tide and try to spot a singel
light shining through the mists of Foulshaw Moss, and years later
I learned from her that the loneliest of the Lake dwellers of the
past were not the people of the hills but the people of the marshes.

The Changing Coast

It is right that any review of the rocks of the Lakes should end
in the mud and sand of the coast for that is where the rocks themselves will end. Moreover, sand and mud are not only the end of
the rock, they are also the beginning. Bomb or no bomb, here on
the coast the sandstones and slates of the future are already being
laid down.

It would be wrong, however, to say that they were taking
shape, for the shape of the dunes can change in a night if there is
a high tide with a wind behind it. Even in more normal times
the dunes show all the signs of weathering by wind and rain—
combes and corries, little gills carved out by trickles of water,
slides and land-slips and screes of sand. They are a working model
of erosion, speeded up for day to day observation.

The dunes for the most part lie in the south-west of Cumberland, since the rivers of Morecambe Bay are without them, and
there are only miserable mole-hill-high specimens along the
coast further north. But on both sides of the Duddon and on
Walney Island, and again around the joint estuary of the Esk,
Mite and Irt, there are great savannahs of sand stretching for miles.
At Haverigg, behind a thirty-foot-high and fifty-yards-solid
sea-wall of dune, the sand is rolled out level and overgrown with
green. This is a dune-turf-land, where the marram grass is replaced by a tight-knit jumper of thyme, tormentil, heart's-ease,
heath and dog violets, bird's-foot trefoil, hare's-foot trefoil, the
small yellow clovers and the white Dutch clover, biting stone-
crop, devil's-bit scabious, hemlock storksbill and a dozen species
of cresses and hawkweeds. To one who recognizes even half these
flowers, the names give out a scent of herby turf, sprinkled with
salt and sizzling with lark-song. On the Lancashire side of the
Duddon, at Askam and Roan Head, the sand is darker and redder,
more mixed with soil, and stained with iron from the old mines.
There is burnet rose, here, with its bleached white flowers and
ebony-black hips, and I have found the yellow dune-pansy—a sea-

side relation of the mountain-pansy of the fells, which, however, is more often blue than yellow.

The dune-flowers, earthy and unostentatious as they are, do keep a kind of check on the sand. But around the Ravenglass estuary the sand is as wild as the Sahara. The rivers of the three most westerly dales—Wasdale, Miterdale and Eskdale—flow more or less parallel each to the other until they reach the lower ground; then the Irt turns south and the Esk turns north and both meet the Mite at Ravenglass where there is an opening to the sea. Between the south-flowing Irt and the sea a long spit of dune-land pushes downward from Drigg, and in the same way a spit pushes upwards from Eskmeals. The Eskmeals dunes are used as a testing range for guns, and are mostly barred off from the public and guarded by Alsatian dogs—though I have heard of an Eskdale archaeologist searching for prehistoric arrow-heads while guns were being fired over her head. But the opposite dunes can be reached by walking along the shore from Drigg or by taking a boat from Ravenglass. The approach by water is much to be preferred, and it is better to go at high tide when you get a longer sail and avoid having to walk across a hundred yards or so of sea mud like black semolina pudding.

You will need permission[1], however, before you can cross over, since these dunes are now a bird-sanctuary, given up, in particular, to the black-headed gulls. About two-thirds of the entire black-headed gull population of England and Wales is believed to breed at Ravenglass or at the smaller colony on the south end of Walney Island. There, too, you will find the other gulls, the common and little terns, and, occasionally, the sandwich, the roseate and the arctic terns. In winter the gulls lose their black heads (except for a spot near the ear) and the land seems populated with common, un-Cumbrian birds—no doubt many of the gulls do migrate to other parts of the country. So that, in spring, the black head of the gull is as sure a sign of the season as the call of a cuckoo, and a much earlier one, too.

When you land on the further side of the estuary you do not at first come acoss the gulls. There are only the enormous dunes, many of them bare of even marram grass. Looking back, you can see the strip of water and Ravenglass village, low and smuggler-like, on the shore, while beyond is the roof-line of the

[1] From the Cumberland County Council.

Wasdale fells—Gable, Scafell and the Screes. You stare from sand to rock, and the water seems more alive than either. You are at the last outpost of land, on the fringe of civilization, as far removed from modern England as if you were in the Hebrides or the western isles of Ireland.

Then you find the gulls—or they find you. They do not readily leave the nest, but as you approach the outer suburbs of the colony one or two outlying pairs take to the wing, and then the rest get up and soon there are thousands flying over your head. The birds swoop down to shoulder-height, sometimes actually striking with wing or beak. They dive and sweep and curl, thousands of them, squawking and squealing, yet never seeming to collide. After the first angry flight some birds settle near their nests, or stand on the sand, screeching, with wings half-stretched-out. But the dipping and diving still goes on. You need an old mackintosh and a cap, for there are droppings everywhere, and a stench comes from the ground. The nests—so close that you can hardly avoid stepping on them—lie under tufts of grass and on little terraces of sand, with thousands of greenish-brown eggs and broken egg-shells and young birds in all stages of development. The fledglings look like small ducklings, and will let you pick them up without showing any sign of nervousness except, perhaps, by wetting your hand. During the war many of the eggs were gathered and sold, and I know of one confectioner whose choco-late-cakes, at that time, had a distinctly fishy flavour. Today, the eggs are protected, though not all escape local collectors, and some may end up on city menus priced as plovers' eggs.

Coastal Erosion

For the most part the dunes give adequate protection against the sea, largely because of the solid banks of shingle which run the whole length of the Lake coast outside Morecambe Bay. At one place, however, there are signs of serious erosion—on the sea-ward side of Walney Island, at a point south of Biggar Bank. Here the island is at its flattest and its narrowest, for on the landward side, opposite Barrow Island, the marshes around Tummer Hill and Biggar Village push to within a quarter of a mile of the open sea. The high tide approaches on both sides, from the Irish Sea and the Walney Channel, threatening one day to cut the island in two. Nor need that day be very distant, for observations carried out by the *Barrow Mail* show that the shore-line is receding, at a measurable rate, month by month.

What is at stake is not just a few hundred acres of farmland or the topography of Lancashire's largest island, but the livelihood of nearly a hundred thousand people. For if the sea does break through at this point it might block the channel and interfere with or even put an end to Barrow Docks and the shipbuilding trade. It was the movement of the glaciers of the Ice Age which opened Walney Channel and Barrow Harbour, and there is a danger that the movements of the present-day tides may close them.

IV

THE LAST CATASTROPHE

As we have just seen, the landscape of the Lakes was shaped largely by a series of catastrophes—volcanic eruption, earthquakes, inundation and glaciation—and the last catastrophe was the coming of man.

He came, like the ice, in a series of invasions the details of which do not concern us now. Those who wish to study them must search elsewhere—either among the transactions of local antiquarian societies, or among the more recent histories of Cumberland and Westmorland that take into account the archaeological discoveries of recent years. Indeed, the pre-history of the area is very confused and conjectural, and a new discovery can lead to considerable revision of theories—our conception of the past changes almost as quickly as our vision of the future. One local archaeologist, having read a manuscript of mine and given it her approval, violently attacked the book when it appeared for expressing just those opinions she herself had held six months earlier. What matters to me is not the may-have-been of pre-history but the mark of the past as it can still be seen in the present.

Now of the people of the past who came to the district, whether to stay or not to stay, many left memorials on the surface of the land—cairns, monoliths, crosses, castles, churches. Others left few visible signs, but their influence is felt in the speech and way of life of those who came after them. All of them, in one way or another, helped to make the Lake area what it is.

The levelling tidal wave of modern civilization is sweeping over the Lakes as over the rest of the world, washing away landmarks and depositing foreign wreckage. Soon the special character of dale life may be obliterated and half-forgotten. But as yet something of that character remains, and the true local accent can still be heard, though it is becoming fainter and fainter.

The Megalith Builders

Archaeologists stare into the mirk of pre-history and see the time-sequence of man's social development—the Early Stone

Age (when the North of England was, in fact, still covered by the ice), the Late Stone Age, Bronze Ages I, II and III, the Iron Age and so on. For me, only one sign is written clearly on the landscape of those early times—that of the Great Stone Circles.

The people who built them came from France and Spain, arriving in our district some time between 1800 and 1500 B.C. They came by sea, spreading along the south-west coast of Cumberland, and along the River Derwent to Keswick and the Eden Valley. In the north-west there are none of the more magnificent remains, like those at Stonehenge, but there are many smaller examples, and nowhere are they so strange and compelling to the imagination as on the moors or the Cumberland coast. The three largest are those at Little Salkeld (Long Meg and her daughters), at Castlerigg near Keswick, and at Swinside near Broughton-in-Furness. There are also smaller circles in various states of preservation, as well as fragments of circles, single monoliths and cairns. Some of them are inaccessible and hard to find; others—like that on Cold Fell between Ennerdale and Calder Bridge—lie at the side of a motor road. They should not all be classified together, because they were built at different times, by different peoples, and served different purposes. Most of the smaller circles enclose burials and this may be true of the larger ones also, though it is hard not to believe that these were gathering-places of some sort.

Of the circles which remain more or less intact some of the stones have toppled over and some have been removed by farmers. The rest must look much as they did to the people who put them up. Long Meg is a fine example of a circle with a gateway and an external menhir—Long Meg herself, a toothless hag of red sandstone. The circle is extremely large, with a farm track driven right across it, and trees standing about. It lies between Cross Fell and the River Eden, and has a slumped resignation very different from the defiant character of the fell-side circles. Castlerigg is not quite so large, but has a kind of internal chamber which, however, may not have been part of the original construction. Swinside is smaller still, and the stones, instead of being spread out, must have been set so close to one another that they touched and made a stone fence.

Of these three circles, Castlerigg has the most magnificent site. It stands on a little knoll with the dip of a valley on nearly

every side and, beyond the dip, a circular rim of mountains.
Standing at the gateway and looking across the circle, you see
the shallow valley of Naddle Beck, very green among the rougher
fell-sides. Parallel is the larger St. John's-in-the-Vale, seen through
a gap in the low Naddle Fell, and beyond it, the Helvellyn range.
To your right, across the valley where Derwentwater lies (unseen
from here) are the fells of Buttermere and Newlands, and behind
you, nearer and more solid, Skiddaw and Saddleback. Its more
immediate surroundings are much tamer—a neat field with a
motor road on two sides of it and a couple of stiles. Passers-by
get out of their cars, climb over the stiles, photograph the circle
and drop sweet-papers in the holy-of-holies.

Swinside, however, still remains comparatively remote and
unvisited, though it can be glimpsed at a distance from the motor
road over Bootle Fell—seeming embedded in its cathedral close
of munched and manured green. It is even possible to force a car
along the road from Broadgate at the risk of breaking the axle.
But for the most part the circle is as hard to reach as it was in
Wordsworth's time.[1] For me, moreover, it has a place in the
memories of boyhood.

There is an age, about fourteen or fifteen, when a restlessness
comes over a boy and his bones seem to be trembling within
him. It may break out in many ways—in games, in religion, in
gangs, in girls. Each generation has its own way of breaking
out which each preceding generation finds hard to understand.
Forty years ago—and so far as I know it may be the same today—
there were at least a few boys to whom it was both a relief and
an exhilaration to get among mountains and wild rocks, alone
or with a friend. It was not primarily the scenery which mattered
—"scenery", in any case, is not a very popular word with the
young. It was more of a desire to walk, to cycle, to climb, to
get out and on and away.

---

[1] It seems to me certain that Wordsworth referred to Swinside in Book II
of *The Prelude* when he speaks of

> " . . . some famed temple where of yore
> The Druids worshipped. . . ."

which he used to visit on horseback excursions from Hawkshead School.
Edward de Selincourt, probably misled by references to Morecambe Bay, thinks
the lines refer to Chapel Island, in the Leven Estuary, but this could scarcely
have seemed, even to Wordsworth, to be connected with the Druids.

I was such a boy, and there was a day when the fit came upon me early one afternoon in November or December. I set off from home not knowing where I was going, and went along the road out of the town, past the football field, towards the Green and Broughton-in-Furness. It had snowed during the week, and there were whips and slashes of snow on the lower hills, but the clouds were too low for me to see if the high fells were more thickly covered. By the time I had reached the Green it had become apparent that the place I was going to was Swinside. I passed through the village and up the hill by Thwaites Church. There was little traffic in those days, and I walked along a grey empty road under a grey and darkening sky.

I turned off the main road and along the track which led to the circle and soon I was out on the open moor. There was snow everywhere, flat and desolate, with tussocks of grass pushing through like hairy warts. The clouds were not far above me, thick and yellow-brown, rubbing on the roof of White Combe. The snow was yellow-brown, too, and you could scarcely tell where snow ended and cloud began. There were shadowy mists and that kind of silence which makes you feel that the air is a solid block. I was thoroughly scared but was determined to go on until I could see the stones. They stand on a little plateau with the smooth fells of the Black Combe range surrounding them on three sides like an ancient earthwork. On the fourth side the land slopes along the line of the beck towards the Duddon Estuary which, however, is not visible from the circle. It is dreary, slovenly country, with not much rock on the surface and the grass sour with bog. And there, at last, I saw the stones, black, huddled and hooded, with the snow mounded against them on the one side. There was no comfort in them, no hint of anything to do with humanity at all. They were as frightening as the moor, yet they were not just a part of it. They were separate, persisting through the centuries in a dumb, motionless struggle. They were in opposition to the moor, struggling against it, just as I was—but they were not on my side. I turned and went as fast as I could down the snowy track to the main road, and walked home towards the friendly glare of the furnaces purring through the mist.

Oddly enough, those neolithic remains do not seem to touch the imagination of the local people. In all the times when I have visited the stones, not once have I seen anyone there. In the early years of the century my father used to pass that way every two or three weeks, carrying patterns and taking measurements for the master tailor who employed him, and not once did he climb over the stile to take a closer look at the stones. Swinside Circle is certainly harder to get at than Long Meg or Castlerigg, but there must be nearly 150,000 people living within twenty or thirty miles of it and I doubt if more than one in fifty has been to see it. Moreover, the destruction which has gone on among these monuments is almost beyond belief. As well as Swinside, there were at least five other circles in South Cumberland—at Annaside, Gutterby, Kirkstones (two) and Standing Stones, Kirksanton. Scarcely anything remains of any of these, though two of the Kirksanton stones, which marked a burial, can be seen from the road just north of the village, looking like giant gate-posts. Other circles have been cleared out of the way by farmers, or the stones have been broken up for making walls and fences. Vanishing circles have been recorded also at four or five places in the north of Cumberland, and one or two near Keswick in addition to that at Castlerigg. One called the Grey Yards on King Harry Fell not far from Carlisle must have been next to the largest in the country. All these seem to have been destroyed in the last two centuries and there may have been others of which we have no record. It is good to be able to tell that one circle, near Seascale, has been reconstructed within sight of the cooling towers of Calder Hall—much of the work having been carried out by boys from Pelham House School, some of whom were probably sent there on account of their own fondness for destruction.

The Early Britons

To distinguish the various cultures of pre-history and to decide at what time each arrived in the district is a job for specialists and not for me. It is made all the more confusing by the fact that the Lakes and Furness were a backward part of the country, still stuck in the Ice Age when primitive man was living in the south, and persisting in Bronze Age ways when the rest of England had advanced to Iron. The poverty of the area meant that old practices were not easily discontinued or old possessions thrown away. When miners in Furness broke into the Old Men's workings, they found two stone axes just as they had been left two thousand years ago—Stone Age tools to dig out Iron Age iron!

Coniston Old Man from Brantwood
The Bowder Stone, Borrowdale

Furness seems to have been comparatively populous in the Bronze Age, with camps or settlements at Aldingham, Walney, Scales and elsewhere, and an important village near Urswick, at what is known as Urswick Stone Walls. There was another pre-Celtic village not far away, near Devoke Water, on the western slopes of Black Combe, with hundreds of burial cairns scattered round it, and there were settlements in other parts of the district, often in wild and bleak places such as the fells above the upper valley of the Calder. These pre-Celtic and early-Celtic tribes were very poor. Though copper was available in the hills they were very slow to turn from stone to bronze. The valley-bottoms were mostly sumps of bog and peat, and the valley-slopes were thickly wooded with oak, chestnut, hazel and birch, so that the people were forced to make their home on the barer hillsides, where they could rear their half-wild stock animals, and grow a little grain when they could scrape together enough soil to plant it in. The camps were often four or five hundred feet above sea-level, exposed to the western winds, with the sea-mists rolling up the dales and the clouds hanging over the fells like a grey thatched roof for days on end. Even today, Devoke Water still lies black and shaly, its shores un-smudged by reed, looking as if the ice-cap had just left it.

Many skeletons found in Bronze Age burials show signs of extensive arthritis.

The Romans

The power of the Roman Empire left its mark, clear and ineradicably, on Cumberland and Westmorland, but its lasting influence was not great. All the other races who settled among the fells were assimilated into the common stock. The Romans were never assimilated—they remained always foreigners.

In fact, the term "race" can hardly be applied to them, for the Roman army of occupation was drawn from all over the Empire, especially from Gaul and Spain. Often the soldiers were not Roman even in the sense in which St. Paul claimed to be so, though at the end of twenty-five years' service they could acquire Roman citizenship if they wished.

For the first twenty years or so of occupation the Romans did not try to subdue the north of Britain since it was clearly of more immediate strategic importance to deal with the Welsh.

Wastwater—Great Gable left of centre
Buttermere

Instead, they made an alliance with the Brigantes, the tribe who controlled practically the whole of the North of England except east Yorkshire. To call them a "tribe" is again, perhaps, misleading for this northern area was split by the Pennines and their outlying spurs into many divisions over some of which the Brigantes can have had little more than a general overlordship, if even that. The late Miss M. C. Fair, the Eskdale archaeologist, insisted that there was no evidence for the presence of Brigantes in West Cumberland. Nevertheless, the alliance was strong enough to save the Romans, at least for a time, from the difficult task of conquest in hill country, and it was the queen of the Brigantes who arrested Caractacus and handed him over to the Romans in chains. When, however, in A.D. 69–70, a faction of the Brigantes revolted, the Romans moved north to impose order on the whole enormous area between the Mersey and the Clyde on the west and the Humber and the Forth on the east.[1]

Their method was to divide the land into districts for administration, and to build forts at road junctions and other commanding places. Each fort held a garrison of five or eight hundred men and could call on the help of the legions if serious trouble broke out. These latter were quartered at Chester and York, so that the working of the scheme depended on good communications northward. On the west the main road ran from Ribchester, via the valleys of the Ribble and the Lune to Penrith and Carlisle. Near Penrith it was joined by the important trans-Pennine route from York, over Stainmore, while in the south it was supplemented by a parallel road running to the west of Bowland Forest and continuing through Lancaster and Kendal. The main part of the task of subduing the north was accomplished by Agricola, who pushed the Roman power right up to the Scottish Highlands and even contemplated an invasion of Ireland. But the size of the area made military occupation very difficult, and this, together with the transfer of one of the British legions to the Continent, led to the withdrawal of troops behind the Tyne-Solway line.

In A.D. 122 or 123 Hadrian began the building of his Wall, with the vallum, fortresses, mile-castles, outposts and the chain of forts along the Cumberland shore of the Solway which are

[1] For a concise and very readable account of these operations see I. A. Richmond: *Roman Britain*—The Pelican History of England, Volume I.

now thought to have formed a kind of wall-less "wall" running as far south as St. Bees.

The Wall is Rome's most tremendous memorial in Britain. It runs along the northern out-banks of the Irthing and the South Tyne, in the muscular country of the Border, among tough-hided, haunch-like escarpments and the long spinal-cords of the fells.

Its purpose, its deliberate carrying out of the job for which it was intended, is obvious, yet it was as much an act of rhetoric as a structure of defence. And even today that rhetoric rouses a response as hundreds of cars drive up to Housesteads on a fine summer afternoon, and parties of schoolchildren run along the hillside to where the ruins are traced on the grass like a plan drawn on a blackboard.

The Wall and the country of the Wall belong in no way to the Lakes but it was behind this defence that the Roman occupation of Cumberland and Westmorland was carried out. The Lakes themselves offered little. Carlisle, in the north of the county, had become a considerable town, while around most of the larger forts on the Wall and at Old Penrith on the main road there grew up villages of shop-keepers, traders and camp-followers. The Roman soldiers frequently married British girls, who lived close to the forts and adopted something of the Roman way of life.

The Lakes, however, had none of this. There was little chance for trade, and the country, from the Roman point of view, did not look inviting. Their policy, therefore, was that of policing rather than of colonizing—of keeping the peace and making the miserable hill farmers pay as much as they could towards the army's upkeep.

But in spite of little hope of profit the Romans took a lot of trouble over this part of the province. From Ambleside (from whence they may have had a rough connecting track along High Street to Brougham) they built a road to Ravenglass on the coast, with a fort at either end of the route and one mid-way at Hard-knott. None of the Border forts has a site to compare with that of Hardknott. It stands on a triangular plateau at the confluence of the valley of the upper Esk and the gill up which runs the track to Hardknott Pass. On the two sea-ward sides the drop is almost sheer. Standing just outside the north-west walls, a Roman soldier could have spat into the river, 400 feet below, if the wind were behind him. And if he turned, and looked updale, he could have seen the main leap of the Esk Falls, white and steady as a pillar of salt. Here the valley opens like a split in a tree-trunk among some of the highest country the Romans ever saw in Britain—Crinkle Crags, Bowfell and the back of the Scafell Range.

On the third side of the triangle the land rises comparatively gently for three or four hundred yards, giving enough room for a parade and exercise ground, and then tilts in another steep rake to the peak of Hardknott Hill. It was a site almost impregnable by the military standards of the second century—but who was going to try to take it in any case? For the men at Hardknott were among the loneliest in the whole Roman Empire, desperately short of company, and relying almost entirely on the port of Ravenglass for their supplies. Even the local girls must have been very scarce.

Ravenglass cannot have been quite as bleak as this, but it was nearly as isolated, the chief link with the imperial forces being by means of the galleys which came up the Irish Sea. It was thought at one time that Ravenglass was to have been the embarkation port for Agricola's projected invasion of Ireland, but this now seems more likely to have been in Galloway, so that the purpose of the station must have been mainly to protect the coast against pirates from Ireland and raiders from Scotland.[1] A patrol route ran northwards to link with the line of forts from Maryport (or St. Bees) to Bowness-on-Solway and the end of the Wall. To the south, the hulk of Black Combe blocked off all reassuring evidence of colonial power, while inland were the thick forests of the lower hills and the long winding march over the two passes to Ambleside. The soldiers tried to get what comfort they could and built a bath-house which stands today though traces of the fort itself have mostly disappeared. The bath-house walls are among the highest still above ground of any Roman building in Britain—a fact probably due to its having been patched up during the Middle Ages for use either as a dwelling-house or a byre. It stands in a narrow strip of plantation, black and dense with conifers, divided from the shore by the railway embankment—a place

---

[1] The fact that both Hardknott and Ribchester were strengthened during the temporary withdrawal from Scotland in the middle of the second century suggests, however, that there had been unrest among the people of the North-west.

of criss-cross beams of sunlight, willowherb in the half-clearings, and sudden tinkles of bird-song among the spruces and firs. At first sight it looks like an abandoned barn—not older it would seem, than the nineteenth century at the most. Yet, when you step inside the walls, you find that you can still follow traces of the central heating system and see the niches which probably held a statue of the goddess of fortune. At Hardknott the Ministry of Works is carrying out a policy of preservation and part-reconstruction similar to that on Hadrian's Wall which has aroused much violent controversy. At Ravenglass the authorities have merely put a sketchy wooden fence round the ruins, and set up a sign saying that it is an Ancient Monument—which, admittedly, is not otherwise obvious. It has even been left to a private landowner to clear away the brambles and nettles which a year or so ago were waist-high in summer. A well-surfaced road has recently been laid down through the wood to Walls Castle, which has been turned into flats, so that the ruins are now passed by dozens or even hundreds of people every day. It seems strange, therefore, that they should remain so neglected and rouse so little interest. Once when I visited them I saw that a small tree had been blown over and was lying propped against one of the walls. A larger tree might have done serious damage. Rome was not built in a day, and it would seem a pity if that which has survived for nearly 2,000 years should be knocked down in a night.

The English

In the centuries which followed the Roman occupation the people living between the Clyde and the Mersey were gathered into the kingdom of Strathclyde. Little is known of this kingdom, though one of the Celtic tribes which lived in the area—the *Cymru*, or Welsh—gave its name to Cumberland. Some early form of Welsh, indeed, was the language of Cumberland when the Romans came and remained long after they had gone, so that you might expect to find a good deal of the Celtic vocabulary embedded in the Lake landscape. In fact, there is very little. A few towns, such as Carlisle and Penrith, retain mainly Celtic names. So do one or two of the fells, such as Helvellyn and Blencathra, while quite a number of the rivers still keep on murmuring in Welsh, including the Eden, the Derwent, the Esk and the Leven. But in the villages, the farms, the clearings and settlements, and in the work and speech of the people, the old Celtic tongue is almost entirely forgotten.

The kingdom of Strathclyde began to disintegrate in the seventh century, by which time two small Anglian kingdoms were established on the north-east coast—Deira round about the Yorkshire Wolds and Bernicia from the Tyne to the Forth. From Bernicia the English infiltrated into Cumberland along the lines of the Eden Valley, and established many settlements on the coast. The western industrial area is full of places with Anglian names: Workington, Harrington, Frizington, Parton, Hensingham and so on. From Deira they spread into South Westmorland, and on to Cartmel and Furness, planting their names in such places as Pennington and Aldingham. Because they were primarily an agricultural people they kept mostly to the lowlands, leaving the fells and the dales to the last remnants of the British. For this reason they are about the least interesting of the early settlers, giving to the people of the two counties only what they have in common with the rest of England. The true "Lake" character came not from the English but from the Norse.

Yet the English introduced a type of monument which is typical of the lowlands of the dale counties though it is not confined to them. This is the sculptured stone, usually a cross, which was set up at market-places, in churchyards or beside graves. There are some fragments of Celtic carving which may be pre-Saxon, but the finest work came in with the English and can be seen in the great cross at Bewcastle[1] near the Border. Bewcastle is many miles away from the Lakes but there is a smaller cross at Irton Church, just below the Eskdale and Wasdale fells. This is a most attractive work, carved with scrolls of fruit, leaves and flowers and with panels of a geometric pattern. It still has its cross-head, with the arms "free" (i.e. not enclosed by a wheel), while the "arm-pits" are cut in a curve which gives grace and movement. It stands in a churchyard, among a group of church, school and one or two other buildings, islanded in fields and seemingly far from any possible churchgoers. Yet a vicar told me that his congregation contained more Bachelors of Science than perhaps that of any other in England.[2]

[1] There is a cast of this cross in Tullie House Museum, Carlisle.
[2] Because of the nearness of the Windscale Atomic Works, of course.

There are several of these Anglian crosses, and more made by the Cumbrians themselves under English instruction. They can be found, of one sort and another, scattered around the county—at Beckermet, St. Bees, Dearham, Aspatria and elsewhere. And there are many fragments in other places—broken bits of shafts built into church walls, fragments of different styles and periods heaped together, wheel-heads set beside shafts to which they do not belong. In many places, too, there is a tradition of a cross which has now entirely disappeared. For the country people seem to have treated the crosses as they treated the megaliths—not even the Christian symbol could save them. One cross, the Giant's Thumb of Penrith, was once used as a pillory, and others became rubbing-stones for cattle.

The Norse Crosses

The Cumbrian cross gradually gave way to a type character-istic of the race which was to come next to the dales—i.e. the Norsemen. There are a good many crosses which show Norse, or Celtic-Norse influence, including the Giant's Grave at Penrith, which has two hog-backs (curved grave-slabs lying not flat but on their sides) and two pillars. But by far the finest as well as the most famous of the Norse sculptures are those at Gosforth.

The Gosforth group consists of the remains of two hog-backs and three crosses, all of about the same period and possibly by the same hand. The standing cross in the churchyard is a most remarkable work. One's first impression is that it is so slender that it might easily snap in two. The lower part of the shaft is round, like a tree-trunk, and undecorated, and then, about four feet from the ground, it breaks out into a pattern, grows narrower, and is cut into four faces. Above, it tapers to a smallish wheel-head cross at the top. It has little of the serenity of the Irton cross, but its detailed carvings tell a complex story. On the east side is a crucifixion—a rather stiff warrior-like Christ watched by a soldier and Mary Magdalene. Above this is a dragon, its body knotted like a hank of knitting wool with a head at either end, while a man stands beside the lower of the two heads, forcing the mouth open with his foot. This, we are told, illustrates the old Norse story of Vidar the Silent, who was to avenge the death of Odin by opening the jaws of the dragon wolf.

Here and elsewhere on this cross Christian and pagan imagery are presented side by side. The stag chased by dogs or wolves is a conventional symbol for Christ, but other figures seem to illustrate stories from the Edda.[1] Such sculptures with their blending of Christian and pagan symbols must have belonged to a time when the Norsemen were converted to Christianity but had not yet forgotten their old mythology and the stories told by the Skalds. It is very likely that they half-believed both Christian and pagan myths simultaneously. Certainly the dragon which is slain by St. Michael on the Dragon Lintel at St. Bees looks more as if he comes from the Edda than from *The Book of Revelation*.

The Norsemen

The race which made the Norse crosses was the last to invade the dales in large numbers, and it was in many ways the most important of all. It has left its names hacked on the fellsides and scotched along the walls of the dales. It has left its language still alive in the dialect. It has left a dale way of life which remained unchanged for centuries. Yet oddly enough this invasion is almost unrecorded. There are a few vague references to Cumberland in the works of early Scandinavian historians and that is about all.

Evidence, none the less, is to be found in place-names. Throughout the ninth and tenth centuries the whole of the north of England endured Scandinavian raids, but the raiders were Danish rather than Norse. The Danes harried the north-east coast and settled in Lincolnshire and Yorkshire. From thence they pressed north into Tyneside and ranged across the country into the British kingdom of Strathclyde, and they are reported to have sacked Carlisle in A.D. 875. In Cumberland and Westmorland, however, the place-names for the most part are not Danish but Norse. There are many places in Norway today the names of which are very similar to those of places in the Lake District[2] and the resemblance is even stronger in the case of Iceland, which seems to be because in Iceland, as in Cumberland, the invading race tended to call the settlements after the chief or warrior who took possession. A great number of place-names in the Lakes contain a Norse surname as part of their etymology. But as we move out of the dales, south into Lancashire, east across the Pennines, or

[1] See W. S. Calverley: *Early Sculptured Crosses of the Diocese of Carlisle*.

[2] E.g. Braithwaite—Braathveit; Seathwaite—Sjöthveit; Micklethwaite—Myklethvet; Rusland—Rüsland.

north into Scotland, the Norse names grow less frequent, giving way to those which are Danish or Saxon. Along the eastern boundary of the district, beside the road from Penrith through Appleby to Kirkby Stephen, there are a large number of place-names ending with the characteristic Danish "by" or "thorpe". This surely shows that the Norse invasion of the dales came not from the north or east or south but from the west—in other words, from the sea.

Invasion by sea was, of course, typical of the Vikings or Norsemen. By the ninth century they had established in Iceland a civilization which was one of the wonders of the Middle Ages. They certainly discovered America and carried their raids as far south as the Mediterranean. From Iceland they swept down, colonizing the Faröes, the Shetlands and the Orkneys and plundering the coasts of Scotland, where they took possession of many of the islands and made some settlements on the mainland. Ireland they seem to have colonized on a larger scale and they set up a kingdom on the Isle of Man. From thence they probably made excursions into Pembrokeshire, since there are a number of Norse place-names around Milford Haven, but their main objective beyond Man was Cumberland.

All this took time—a matter of generations rather than years. The Norsemen, by now, were much influenced by the Celts, with whom they had mixed and married, and from whom they had learnt some of the gentler arts of civilization and also, probably, something of Christianity. They were no longer merely raiders or barbarians. So that when they looked east from Snaefell across the thirty miles of sea to the skyline of Cumberland, they were thinking not of loot but of a country to settle in. And when eventually they set foot on the Cumberland coast, they found a land of narrow dales, divided one from another by high ridges, well suited to the life of small individualistic communities such as they were used to. It was on a smaller scale than Iceland, but less severe, and in each of the dales there was a strip of land potentially far more fertile than the barren acres of the subarctic.[1] It was a cosier, more friendly country. They must have felt at home almost at once.

Nor is it likely that they met with great opposition. The English

[1] It is possible, however, that in the ninth century the climate of Iceland was warmer than it is today.

were settled in the lowlands along the Solway, but there were not many of them south of St. Bees Head. The British tribes which still remained in the hills had been dwindling for centuries, though north of the Duddon they had made an alliance with the Scottish Lowlanders and revived the old kingdom of Cumbria or Strathclyde. In A.D. 945, however, this came to an end when the Cumbrians, under the command of King Dunmail, were defeated by the Saxon King Edmund. Tradition points to Dunmail Raise, the pass between Thirlmere and Grasmere, as the field of battle and the site of the king's grave, though, in fact, he died at Rome thirty years later.

We cannot be certain what happened to the Cumbrians after this. Maybe some of them emigrated to Wales; maybe the survivors were allowed to linger on among the mountains. Certainly they would be in no state to offer much resistance to the Norsemen. By the twelfth century we may take it for granted that the dales were inhabited by a mixed race, predominantly Norse in blood and custom, and speaking a Norse dialect probably incomprehensible in the rest of England.

The Norse Heritage

Once the Vikings were settled in the dales neither Celt nor Scot nor Englishman could shift them. As in Iceland, the nature of the terrain encouraged them to set up small, self-contained, dale communities loosely linked one with the other. In Iceland their society had been aristocratic, because it needed capital to set up in such a barren country and at such a distance from the home base. In Cumberland the pattern seems to have been that of isolated groups where each family either owned its own farm or occupied it by some kind of hereditary tenancy. The Cumberland "statesman" or "estatesman" of Wordsworth's day and even later may, perhaps, be a link with the Norse system of land tenure, though it must be emphasized that this cannot possibly be proved. And, in any case, the various kinds of customary tenant-right differed so much from farm to farm that the splendid republican figure of the "statesman" must be regarded to some extent as a romantic simplification.[1]

In fact, it may be merely romantic to pretend to recognize any-

[1] See especially: *The Lake Counties: 1500–1830. A Social and Economic History*, by C. M. L. Bouch and G. P. Jones.

thing at all of the Norseman in the character of the present-day dalesman. Yet his love of country sports, especially of wrestling, goes back, if not to the times of the Norsemen, at least to the times of men who lived much as the Norsemen had lived.

And though, as far as I know, none of the old Icelandic tales has come down to us in our folk-lore, I like to fancy that I can see something of the gesture and swagger of the sagas in the tall stories which have long been popular with Cumbrians. Exaggeration is a convention in northern conversation which often bewilders southerners. Will Ritson, landlord of the Wasdale Head Inn in the last century was famous for such stories. He told of an eagle with a broken wing which was put in a chicken run and mated with a foxhound bitch to breed winged hounds that hunted along the screes. It is a long way from that story to the sagas, but the fantastic touch is there and the homely touch, too.

It is said of Will Ritson that he entered a competition at the dale sports for the man who could tell the biggest lie, but when it came to his turn he asked to withdraw.

"Why?" he was asked.

"Because I cannot tell a lie." [1]

He won. And there, too, is the shrewdness which was often found in the Norse tales.

But these are dim relics of the Norsemen, romantic images blurred by the mist. It is hard to be sure to what extent the Lake population, even in Wordsworth's time, derived directly from Norse ancestry, while the population of today is almost as mixed as that of the residential suburbs of a seaside holiday town.

Yet there are still signs which cannot be forgotten since they are engraved across the landscape like the names on a map. Fell, scar, scree, gill, tarn, beck—these Norse words at once name the landscape and bring it to the eye. They make sure that the Lake scene will not only look different from any other in England but will sound different too. Their synonyms have nothing like the same force—no one could confuse a fell with a hill. They belong so particularly to the north that a southerner uses them almost self-consciously, as if in inverted commas, while they come as easy as whistling to the lips of the Cumberland man. There are

---

[1] It was the traditional—and inaccurate—boast of Wasdale that it possessed "the highest mountain, the deepest lake, the smallest church and the oldest bell," the fourth of these claims being later amended to "the biggest liar".

others, not quite so familiar, which have the same expressiveness: pike, gable, knot, mire, force (a waterfall), nab (a projection, as in Nab Scar on Rydal and Nab Cottage where De Quincey lived for a time). Some topographical terms have more than one meaning. Hawes or hause or hows, for instance, may be derived from Old Norse *hals*, a neck or pass (e.g. Esk Hause), or from *haugr*, a hill or mound (Skiddaw), or again it may be related to the northern dialect word, *haugh* which usually means the flat alluvial meadows beside a river.

Many of these Norse words are also known as common suffixes or prefixes in place-names—*thwaite*, a clearing, the best known of all. There must be a hundred places in the Lake District the names of which end in *thwaite*, as well as a large number of surnames— my own middle name being Cornthwaite. Then there is *biggin* (a building), *keld* (a spring), *wath* (a ford as in Langwathby), *holm* (an island, or a piece of land half-surrounded by a stream as in Holmrook or Herbertholm, the old name for St. Herbert's Island in Derwentwater), *thorpe* (farm or hamlet: Crackenthorpe, the home of Wordsworth's maternal great-grandparents), *scales* (*skali*, a shepherd's summer-hut; Seascale, Portinscale), *wick* (*vik*, a creek or bay—the *Vik*ings were the "creek-men"), *seat* (*sætr*, a summer-pasture farm or shieling: Seatoller).

Seat, when it is a suffix, is often changed to "side"—as in Swinside and Ambleside—and this may lead to confusion. On one of the bleakest stretches of the south Cumberland coast there is a very old farming settlement at the mouth of the large beck which flows from the slopes of Black Combe and through the village of Bootle. This settlement was named from the Old Norse personal name Einarr and so became Einarr's Sætr, and through various corruptions (Aynerset, Andersetta, Anerset, etc.[1]) to Annaside. The beck, naturally enough, took its name from the settlement and became Annaside Beck. But recently, people have begun mistakenly to presume that the settlement took its name from the beck, since Annaside looks as if it means "beside the Anna", so that in the last few years Annaside Beck has appeared on maps pretentiously swollen into "The River Annas".[2]

[1] See: *The Place-Names of Cumberland*, Cambridge University Press.
[2] A somewhat similar inflation of a name has occurred in the case of Haverigg Pool, the beck which drains Whicham Valley and enters the sea at the mouth of the Duddon. During the last century this was jokingly referred to as "the River

There are many other Norse words too deeply grafted into the local names to be easily recognizable, and others—suffixes such as *land* or *ness* (a promontory)—which may come either from Old Norse or from Old English, but where the other part of the name suggests a Norse derivation. Even such English-looking words as "mere" and "water" are often found linked to Scandinavian surnames. Buttermere, Windermere, Grasmere, Ullswater, Elterwater and Thurston Water (the old name for Coniston Lake) have been thought to contain respectively the Scandinavian names of Buthar, Windar, Gris (meaning "swine"), Ulf (a wolf), Eldir and Thorstein.

The identity of those one-time landlords—if they were landlords—is in doubt, but surely there can be no doubt of each lake's own identity as a *lake*. Yet, this doubt does apparently exist in the minds of those people who now label them "*Lake* Windermere", "*Lake* Buttermere", and so on. A certain excuse for the tautology can be made in the case of Windermere, since we need to differentiate between the lake and the town, though it would be better to speak of "Windermere Lake" and "Windermere Town", but no one can excuse such ridiculous clumsiness as "Lake Derwentwater" and "Lake Ullswater". Strictly speaking, the map gives the name "Lake" to only one of the lakes—i.e. Bassenthwaite.[1] All the rest are either "waters" or "meres". Nevertheless it seems to me over-pedantic to object to the use of "Coniston Lake" (the term which is always used by the village people themselves) or "Ennerdale Lake". The trouble arises when the words are twisted round and become "Lake Coniston", a term which I find just as annoying as the tautological "Lake Windermere" or "Lake Derwentwater". For this is entirely against the tradition of Cumberland and Westmorland nomenclature. We always put the plain topographical term second—"fell", "beck", "dale", "thwaite" and so on. Then we set in front of this the term which describes it or the surname with which it is associated. Thus we say "Scafell" (bald fell) and not Fell-sca, Troutbeck and not Beck-trout, Langdale, Braithwaite (broad thwaite) and so on.

Lazy" and that name is now solemnly used by local councillors as being more proper than the vulgar Haverigg Pool.

[1] But "Bassenthwaite Lake" is not only the name of the lake but the name of the old station on the Workington–Penrith railway, so one day, to avoid confusion with the station, I expect to read of "Lake Bassenthwaite Lake."

The habit of reversing the natural order of Lake names may have been caught from the Americans (Lake Michigan, etc.) or even from foreign travel. Certainly it seems to appear most frequently in tourist brochures, railway posters and advertisements for holiday accommodation. Maybe "Lake Windermere" sounds a more fashionable spot than just "Windermere." Or maybe the advertisers fear that the public will not know there *is* a lake. But, again, it may have been caught from the Scots (Loch Ness, Ben Nevis, Glengarry, etc.). It is certainly this Scottish or Celtic accent which appealed to the ear of John Ruskin of Coniston who was not satisfied with plain Tom Gill as the name of the little ravine in Yewdale which carries off the overflow from the present-day Tarn Hows. He re-named it, therefore, with the fanciful, sham-Balmoral name of "Glen Mary" and this, unfortunately, has caught on with the public.

Now it might seem that Tarn Hows itself is a contradiction of what I have called the typical practice of putting the descriptive term first and the topographical term second. But this is not so. For "Tarn Hows" is not the name of the tarn at all. Strictly speaking, the tarn, which is one of the most popular parking places in the Lakes, has no name at all, being merely an artificial pond created by damming up a stream and a few swampy pools.[1] "Tarn Hows", in fact, applies not to the tarn but to the hows or hill above it—i.e. it is not "the tarn beside the hill" but "the hill beside the tarn". On this analogy "Lake Windermere" clearly refers to the town and not the lake!

Sometimes the names have changed so much in the course of time that it is hard to suspect that they once had a Scandinavian ring. Who would have thought that Dolly Waggon Pike did not come out of a typical English folk-song? Moreover, as I write, I can look out of my window to a small knott of Silurian rock. It is built over now, being the oldest part of a market village which, when industry came to South Cumberland, became the suburbs of the new town. The slates pile up each behind the other, in sharp angles of roof, dormer window and gable end. From hidden plots of garden the tops of elders and apple trees puff out a green smoke among the smokeless chimneys of summer. At the very peak of the hill is a former nonconformist chapel, in buff sandstone, now turned into a bakery. The drab nineteenth-

[1] Hence the term "To the Tarns" on the signposts.

century houses are heaped and jumbled by the heave of the hill to make a mining-town St. Michael's Mount. Its name is Holborn Hill, and it was by this name that Millom was known when first it began to grow into a town. The name, of course, looks like a reference to London, and there are many such references, and references to places as far apart as California, Gibraltar, and Jericho to be found among the farms of the district. But though Holborn Hill cannot be traced back beyond the eighteenth century, and hence survives in no early form, it seems at least possible that it may preserve the memory of Hallbjörn, an old Viking.

And if the place-names record the dead Norsemen as on a tombstone, the dialect still keeps their language at least half alive. It is not, however, true to say that there is one dialect in the district, for the speech of the coastal dales varies considerably from that of Westmorland or even of Furness. The colliery district of Whitehaven and Workington has a dialect quite of its own which, to my ears, sounds like a cross between Cumberland and Tyneside, while Barrow-in-Furness speaks a language not easily distinguishable from that of any industrial town of the North West.

The true dale dialects are full of Norse words and have a clicking, cracking, harshly-melodious tune in which nearly all the vowels are diphthongs or triphthongs. In fact, in three words out of four the old dalesman seems to use a sound which can perhaps be suggested by "ee-y-an", though there are slight variations of colour which differentiate the vowel. Thus a farmer speaking to me of an unsuccessful fox-hunt said:

"Nee-y-ah scee-y-ant at ee-y-al", and there was no doubt whatever that he meant "No scent at all".

The dialect is dying out, and it is no good either denying this, lamenting it or trying to prevent it. In any case dialect is not held in much honour by the ordinary countryman since it is associated in his mind with poor education and the status of the farm labourer. So that the people who really value the dialect are precisely those who do not normally speak it. For this reason, though I am a member of the Lakeland Dialect Society and appreciate the work of recording and studying the dialect, I see little use in trying to preserve it. An attempt has been made, for instance, to encourage the writing of essays or stories in dialect among the children of the country schools. I have seen some of these productions which make me feel that the children think of dialect writing purely in terms of reproducing local pronunciation by means of conventional phonetic spelling. Thus we get a script bristling with apostrophes, dropped "g"s and "h"s and uncouth vowels—"t'" and "an'" and "yam" and "steeän" and "mudder"—but with scarcely a trace of the true dialect vocabulary. Obviously the duller child—who, let us face it, is the one most likely to use the dialect—finds it hard enough to learn to spell normal English without having to tackle these orthographical perversions.[1] The brighter child, on the other hand, soon learns the trick of translating his words into the sham vernacular, but in doing so he is not getting to know the dialect better: he is doing precisely the opposite. He is moving away from it; he is learning to think of it as odd, as old-fashioned, as not for people like him. A modified form of dialect will no doubt persist as a regional accent and help to give variety of colour to the sound of England, but dialect as a local language is doomed to disappear. It is notable, for instance, that the speech of young men and women from the towns and cities of almost any part of Great Britain, though it may differ enormously in accent and pronunciation, is made up of the same vocabulary and idiom. Dialect is already becoming not the language of the people but a literary language evolved from the vernacular of the past. And since Cumberland has no dialect writer of importance we should be thankful that at least part of our old vocabulary remains active and alive in the place-names and the language of topography.

---

[1] On the very day of writing the above I saw the Cumbrian county anthem recorded in a schoolgirl's essay as "Dear Ken John Peel".

Seathwaite in Borrowdale

V

THE BORDER WARS

LOOKING north from almost any point on the southern coast of Cumberland, you will find the distant view blocked off by St. Bees Head—that "sapphire promontory", as Thomas Carlyle called it, remembering it as seen from the Dumfriesshire hills. But once you go past St. Bees, the sky opens out above the Solway and you see the long Mulberry Harbour of Galloway stretching from Criffell to Whithorn and Drummore, seemingly foreign-looking and as if beyond the seas. And at Carlisle you feel that you are no longer in England, nor yet in Scotland, but in the capital of a Debatable Land, always in a state of uneasy Border truce. As you come out of the station you see the law courts, circular and squat—like rooks in a chess-set. They were built in the nineteenth century, as was much of the gothic architecture of the city, but the Border watchfulness hangs over them like a curse.

In the Lake District proper it is possible to forget that Cumberland is a Border County. The warfare which swished backward and forward across the Solway for three or four centuries left it almost untouched, though it made its mark in the lowlands and the coast. It is not part of the purpose of this book to try to tell the complex history of the Border counties. Perhaps it will be enough to say that the wars fell roughly into two periods, in the first of which the boundaries between England and Scotland were still undetermined, while in the second, they had been settled, but raids and counter-raids went on.

Soon after the Norman Conquest King Malcolm of Scotland seized the land north of the Duddon, and in 1092 William Rufus captured Carlisle—or rather the ruins of it, left by the Danish raid of 200 years earlier—and built Carlisle Castle. From then onwards the English kings regarded Cumberland as part of their dominion though the people cannot have been quite sure to which country they belonged. In church affairs, for instance, the Bishop of Glasgow, the Archbishop of York and the Archdeacon of Richmond all claimed authority in the area,[1] and it was to clear up this confusion that Henry I created the diocese of Carlisle in 1133. (Incidentally, this included only the northern parts of the two counties—all Cumberland south of Workington, together with South Westmorland, and Furness and Cartmel in Lancashire, being left in the Archdeaconry of Richmond. Not until 1856 were these southern parishes annexed by the Carlisle diocese, so that the nearness of the Border acted for centuries as a dividing influence on the Lake area.) During the reign of Stephen, Henry I's successor, the Scots once again overran Cumberland and Westmorland, and King David of Scotland set up residence in Carlisle. But Stephen and David both died round the middle of the twelfth century and Henry II had little difficulty in wresting the territory from the hands of the boy Malcolm who succeeded David.

For a long time the Scottish kings continued to claim the northern part of Cumberland, but in the thirteenth century understanding between the countries improved, and soon after he came to the throne Edward I stayed in Carlisle, visited Lanercost Priory and hunted in Inglewood Forest. These years of frontier warfare were unsettled, murderous and cruel, though compared with the years which followed they were almost peaceful. The people on either side of the Border knew at least when there was a war on and when there was not.

Throughout this time the king-pin of defence was Carlisle Castle, though all the castles built to protect the newly-established Norman baronies helped in the defence of the Border. In the north there were Carlisle, Liddell Strength, and Naworth. Along the Eden Valley there were Brougham and Appleby, commanding fords over the Eamont and the Eden; Brough, commanding the pass over Stainmore into Yorkshire; and Pendragon, in the lost, upper valley of the river, on the way to Wensleydale. Appleby, like Brough, now stands on the main road linking the A6 to Scotch Corner, but by a happy accident the road runs one side of the river and the castle lies on the other. Thus the town lives a double life. North of the Eden it is strung out along the scorching road with a skirting-board of public-houses, snack-bars and petrol-stations. South of the river it is as sedate as a cathedral close—church, cloister, streets and market-

[1] See: *The Lake Counties: 1500–1830*, C. M. L. Bouch and G. P. Jones.

place making up the neatest, and quite probably the smallest, county town in England.[1]

To the west, at Egremont and Cockermouth, there were castles of a rather different type, with neither pele tower nor keep, while in the south, commanding the shallow valleys which run down to Morecambe Bay, was the castle of Kendal. These three, however, can have played little part in the defence of the Border.

I confess that I do not feel much love for the castles. They were, from the beginning, places of oppression, outposts of an usurping, foreign aristocracy. They brought little but misery to the local people during the first few hundred years of their existence. Yet the three which belong specifically to the Lake area all have a grim grandeur about them. And, oddly enough, all lie near the junction of the slate with the limestone. Kendal is splendid in its situation. Cockermouth, still partly inhabited, stands beside the confluence of the Cocker with the Derwent, near the spot where the five-year-old Wordsworth "made one long bathing of a summer's day." It is richly embowered, as the fifty-five-year-old Words-worth might have said, in trees and tree-reflecting water, but, unlike Appleby Castle, it has imposed no sedateness on the town at its foot. From one view, the ventilators and turrets of a brewery mingle with the castle battlements in an anachronistic, rococo fantasy.

Yet, of the three lake castles, it is Egremont which is the most romantic of all, for, like Cockermouth, it is in limestone country and here the rock yields iron-ore. Egremont rises above a town which has known the grimmest of the Border struggles of this century and the last—the struggle of man with the rock and with unemployment and poverty. The castle grounds are now a public park. You can walk along paths and inspect the herring-bone masonry and see the yellow groundsel growing on the red stone—for the castle is built not of the rock on which it stands but of sandstone presumably from St. Bees.

Inland are Pillar and the Ennerdale Fells, humped and rounded; west, the Irish Sea and the Isle of Man; south, Windscale and Calder Hall where many of the Egremont people work. Below, in scoops and moats, are the old, worked-out mines, with heaps of rubble red as the castle walls. To those who have grown up in the new, post-war prosperity, the Slump seems as remote as

[1] Westmorland's administration centre, however, is at Kendal.

the Border Wars. To others, only a few years older, the scars of the 'twenties are as deep as any left by the raiding Scots.

The Scottish Wars of Independence

Towards the end of the thirteenth century the Scots found a new leader in William Wallace, who in 1298 ravaged the northern counties as far south as Durham. Edward I took an army over the Border and defeated the Scots at Falkirk, and Wallace was betrayed and beheaded. But then Robert Bruce appeared. Edward, who was already mortally ill, gathered together another army, but died at Burgh-by-Sands on the Solway, with only a mile or so of water between him and the country he had come to conquer.

The second of the Edwards had little of his father's toughness or ability. He advanced into Scotland as far as Stirling and was overwhelmingly defeated by Robert Bruce at Bannockburn just south of the city. The northern counties lay open to the invaders, who besieged Carlisle Castle several times though without success. But the castle was now of little importance, for the aim of the Scots was not to occupy the land but to pillage and plunder.

This period was the most ferocious in the whole history of the Border. Farms and churches were burned, cattle driven off and slaughtered, women raped, children impaled on spikes, abbeys plundered, monks murdered, nuns stripped and violated. The northern abbeys suffered most, and even the fact that Robert Bruce's father was buried at Holme Cultram failed to protect it. Moreover, the foraging bands began to move further afield. In 1319 the Bruce burnt the bishop's palace at Rose Castle, went south to Furness (where the Abbot paid ransom), ravaged around Cartmel, crossed the Morecambe Bay sands, burnt Lancaster and then returned to Scotland.

It soon became obvious that the old line of defence, based on Carlisle and the other castles, was no longer adequate. Cockermouth, Naworth, Millom and Penrith were strengthened and, in some cases, given permanent garrisons, though such a castle as Penrith was designed only to give temporary shelter until help could be brought from Carlisle.

Gradually, however, the barons and landowners began to take the initiative. They realised that what they were up against was not large-scale, organized warfare but a series of short, improvised raids. What was needed was a system of many small local defences, where each landowner, with his family and tenants, could hold out for a day or two, or even for an hour or two, for the raiders could not afford to waste time and there was little danger of a long siege. Wooden buildings, of course, were useless—they went down before fire every time.

So the pele towers came into being. They are, for the most part, oblong or square buildings, with walls five to ten feet thick. The general plan was that of a basement with two or three storeys above, the upper floor being divided by partitions into various apartments. The entrance was by a low doorway that led to the basement, so giving no chance for invaders to rush in. As a defence against fire, the door itself was heavily barred and studded with iron. And if the invaders managed to break into the basement they then found that they had to fight their way up a narrow twisting staircase to reach the people on the floors above.

These towers were given almost entirely to defence with little thought of comfort or elegance. The lower windows were nothing but slits, though upstairs, in the women's rooms, there might be small double windows decorated with trefoils and the like which became more elaborate as the centuries passed on and peace was more assured. But the general appearance is of gaunt, massive strength, stubborn and dour.

The building of towers and castles and the fortifying of manor houses was so widespread in the fourteenth century that I am tempted to quote the names of some of these places merely to show how they sprang up all over the two counties, along the Border, the coast, and the lower valleys, everywhere, in fact, except in the higher dales whose very inaccessibility was a defence. There were, then, Naworth, Scaleby, Rose, Hutton-in-Forest, Yanwath, Dacre, Irton, Muncaster, Millom, Piel, Wraysholme, Levens, Sizergh, Burneside, Kentmere, Beetham, Hazelslack, Arnside and many others.

Some of these names will be unfamiliar even to those who know the district well. They are spread over the whole area and many of them belong to the valleys round Morecambe Bay which might have been thought comparatively safe from the Scots. Only two of the towers in that list are in total ruins—Arnside and Piel. The latter, magnificently sited on a small island in Walney Channel, served chiefly to protect the harbour used by the monks of Furness. Some of the castles have become mansions.

Naworth, rebuilt after a fire in the nineteenth century, became the home of one of the most formidable women politicians of the late Victorian and Edwardian Ages, Rosalynd, Countess of Carlisle: liberal, teetotaller, Home Ruler, pro-Boer and advocate of women's suffrage. It is now turned into flats. But most of the peles have become farms, though often the present farm-house is a new building and the old pele is used as a barn or is allowed to stand as a ruin. A good example can be seen from the train at Wraysholme on the old Furness railway line between Cark-in-Cartmel and Kent's Bank.

Again, many of the farms were once strengthened for defence, even though they may not have attained the dignity of a pele. Such typical dale farms as Dalegarth Hall in Eskdale and Coniston Old Hall on the bank of the lake, were once fortified. Today, with their large round chimneys like a ship's funnel they look rather like the dalesman's equivalent in slate of the Elizabethan manor house of brick and half-timbering. In one or two districts, also, the church was used as a place of refuge during raids, Burgh-by-Sands on the Solway and Great Salkeld on the Eden being the most notable, each with narrow windows, set high from the ground, and a thick and immensely strong tower. Great Salkeld, in fact, is more or less a pele tower with nave attached.

Some of the church towers were used, also, as sites for beacon fires.[1] For in the fifteenth century there was developed the great system of beacons to give warning of the Scottish raids—"the red glow on Skiddaw warned the burghers of Carlisle". But Skiddaw is not really a good place for a beacon. It is too high and remote. More suitable are the small accessible hills, six or seven hundred feet high, in the more populous lowlands and along the coast.

There is a number of such in the district, still bearing the name of Beacon Hill, the most famous being at Penrith, where Wordsworth found what he thought was the name of a murderer[2] cut

[1] The late Miss Fair told me that she could remember having seen, some sixty years ago, traces of stains from a beacon fire on the church tower at Dearham.

[2] The letters were, in fact, the initials of the murdered man, Thomas Parker. The real murderer, who was hanged at Carlisle, was called Thomas Nicholson, so that I like to think that perhaps an ancestor of mine played his part, however indirectly, in inspiring one of the most sublime passages in *The Prelude*—Book XII, line 208 onwards.

on the turf near the site of an old gibbet. The beacons were linked together almost as thoroughly as A.R.P. warnings during the last war, and covered the whole area, from Bewcastle in the north, to Black Combe, Rampside in Furness and Farleton Fell in the south of Westmorland. More recently they have been lit again for jubilees and coronations, together with bonfires on the top of Scafell Pike, Coniston Old Man and elsewhere. At such times we have all looked forward to a blaze along the skyline that would dim the Northern Lights, but each time, within my experience, mist and low cloud have blotted out all but the nearest. My father, however, remembered having counted over thirty at the coronation of King Edward VII.

The Border Raids

In the time of Henry VIII, the Battle of Flodden, and later that of Solway Moss, put an end to the long years of warfare and large-scale raids. The southern part of the two counties now began to settle down, and the new castles and manors of the fifteenth and sixteenth centuries looked more like houses and less like pill-boxes. But it was long before the Border really became peaceful and there now began the struggle for the Debatable Land, the tract between the Esk and the Sark, in which the Armstrongs and Grahams began to set up a law for themselves. This was the time of the "cattle-reivers", when the lady of the house, having run out of food, would serve up a pair of spurs on a dinner-dish. This was the time, also, of Kinmont Willie and the Border ballads.

Yet all this made little mark on the Lakes. Wordsworth almost completely ignored the romantic folk-lore of the ballads, though he was brought up on the edge of Inglewood Forest, far nearer the Border than was Scott at Edinburgh. Nor were the Lakes greatly troubled by the Civil War of the seventeenth century, though Carlisle suffered one of the most terrible sieges in English history, and the royalist castles, in places as far apart as Appleby and Millom, got their old walls knocked about a bit. The two Jacobite invasions of 1715 and 1745, though they caused great furore in Carlisle, Penrith and Appleby, by-passed the Lakes altogether, and, after the Duke of Cumberland had chased Charles Edward back over Shap, the county from which he took his title had no more to fear from the Scots.

The Last Invasion

Yet the '45 was not quite the last invasion of Cumberland. There was one more which—if certain known or suspected attempts of the Germans are not taken into account—must be the last time enemy forces ever landed in any part of England.

John Paul Jones, like the earlier invaders, was a Scot, born in Kirkcudbrightshire. As a lad he came to Whitehaven to be apprenticed to ship-building, but he did not care for the place and took his chance to sail for the New World. There he became an American citizen, and in the War of Independence had command of a privateer, *The Ranger*, which was equipped at Nantes for an expedition against England. In the early morning of the 23rd April 1778 he sailed into Whitehaven harbour and began to set fire to shipping. The alarm was given, however, and the ship's crew had to pull away from the shore, and it was only through his knowledge of the harbour that Jones was able to pilot the ship out to sea before the guns of the battery were brought to bear on him.

VI

HOW BEAUTIFUL UPON THE MOUNTAINS

CHRISTIANITY first came to the north with the Roman soldiers, some of whom were believers, though they cannot have made many converts among the native Cumbrians who mostly continued to worship their Celtic gods. Towards the end of the Roman occupation, St. Ninian, [1] who by tradition was born on the banks of Solway, carried out an evangelical campaign in south-west Scotland from a centre at Whithorn, and it is just possible that he may have set up a similar mission close to the Romano-British settlement at Brougham, where the parish church is still called Ninekirks. He must, in any case, have passed along the roads of Cumberland and Westmorland on his way to Rome where, according to Bede, he was instructed.

St. Kentigern

After the fall of the Roman Empire any form of Christian organisation in England crumbled and decayed. A faint after-glow of the faith may have smouldered on in some of the British villages round the old Roman camps but the people of the mountains remained wholly pagan. Yet this was the time when the Celtic Church burned at its brightest—the Church of the holy islands, Iona, Mona, Lindisfarne. In the archipelagoes of the west, in Ireland, in Scotland, and to a lesser extent down the western edge of England and Wales, there flourished a civilization which we can now see only as we see a sunken church through the water of low tide. Little of it remains today but jewellery, illuminated manuscripts and carved stones, but in its own times, together with the Church of Rome and the Church of Byzantium, it was one of the three main branches of Christendom.

[1] Bede: *Ecclesiastical History* (*Everyman* translation)
"For the southern Picts, who dwell on this side of those mountains, had long before [i.e. before the coming of St. Columba] forsaken the errors of idolatry, and embraced the truth, by the preaching of Ninias, a most reverend bishop and holy man of the British nation."

The Church of St. Columba and St. Patrick had already begun its mission to the English when St. Cuthbert took his grasp on Northumberland and Durham, and it is possible that Patrick himself may have visited Cumberland towards the end of the fifth century. But it was from Scotland rather than from Ireland that the renewed faith is believed to have come, and the leader of the missionary movement was St. Kentigern, who is also known as Mungo, the patron saint of Glasgow. Next to nothing about Kentigern's ministry in Cumberland can be taken as certain fact. Most of what we know or think we know may be no more than legend, though the legend has itself become part of our history and helped to shape it.

According, then, to a biography written six hundred years after Kentigern's death by Jocelyn, a monk of Furness Abbey, the saint's mother was a girl belonging to one of the royal families of Scotland. In imitation of Our Lady she vowed herself to virginity and turned down Ewen, a chieftain, who wanted to marry her. Her father, bitterly angry, sent her to be a servant at a farm by the Solway or in the Lowland hills, where Ewen followed and seduced her by treachery or by force.

When it was discovered that she was with child she was condemned to death, according to the custom of her tribe. She was carried to the top of the hill in the Lammermuirs, tied to a chariot, and sent rolling down the steep slopes. As if by a miracle the chariot survived without being dashed to pieces. The girl was unhurt and it seemed that the angels must have borne her up and kept her from harm. But the justices were not satisfied, saying that she had saved herself by witchcraft and must therefore die a witch's death by water. So she was taken down to the sea, put into a small boat made of hides, and pushed out on the tide without oar or rudder. The coracle was swept out to sea and at dawn the girl was cast on the northern shore of the Firth of Forth, and there, beside a shepherd's fire, she gave birth to her child. There was not even a manger to lay him in, nor straw for warmth, but it was the shepherds who first found him as once before they had found another Child—the hagiologists did not miss the parallel. This is said to have been in the year 518.[1]

This boisterous treatment had no harmful effect on the child.

[1] See: *St. Kentigern and St. Herbert*, by H. D. Rawnsley, a rare pamphlet of much charm.

He was brought up and taught by St. Silvanus, a hermit who lived nearby, and became Bishop of Glasgow at the age of twenty-five, by which time he was already famed for his gentleness, courtesy and eloquence. He continued his work with zeal until a time came when the Christians were persecuted in Scotland and he had to flee to Wales, to his friend and fellow bishop, St. David. It was on his journey to Wales that Kentigern first passed through Cumberland, and Jocelyn of Furness says that at Carlisle "he heard that many among the mountains were given to idolatry and ignorant of divine law; thither he turned aside, and, God helping him and confirming the Word by signs following, he converted to the Christian religion many from a strange belief and others who were erroneous in the faith." [1]

The monk then cries out: "Oh, how beautiful upon the mountains were the feet of him . . . that brought good tidings of good, that published salvation, that said unto Zion, thy God reigneth." [2] According to tradition, Kentigern set up his cross at Crosthwaite, and preached in his own tongue (i.e. some form of Welsh) to a congregation of about five hundred and ninety. [3] The present church of Crosthwaite, which dates mostly from the fifteenth century, is the parish church of Keswick—a stubborn, squat-towered building with no futile perkiness about it, yet quite unawed at having Skiddaw almost in its churchyard. The eleven-year-old John Ruskin attended a service at Crosthwaite just to get a glimpse of Southey. Modern sightseers visit the church to see Southey's grave, without much idea why they do so. Canon Rawnsley, one of the founders of the National Trust, was vicar there, so that Crosthwaite might reasonably claim to be the parish church of the Lakes National Park.

It would seem that the mountains did not prove stony ground, for churches sprang up in the path of the saint and today there remain eight dedicated to his honour. Jocelyn of Furness says that these are all at places where he rested, preached and baptized, and this may not be impossible, since they are all in the upper half of Cumberland, and most of them are close to a well, except for Crosthwaite, which is close to the river. Irthington and Grinsdale are in the north, near the Roman road, the natural line of approach

[1] Quoted from Rawnsley's *St. Kentigern.*
[2] *Ibid.*
[3] See: *The Lake Counties: 1500–1830,* C. M. L. Bouch and G. M. P. Jones.

while Caldbeck, Castle Sowerby, Mungrisdale[1] and Crosthwaite
are all to be found around the Skiddaw group of fells. Aspatria
and Bromfield lie between Keswick and the coast, well off the
main north–south route, but they may be brought into Kentigern's itinerary if you presume that he travelled from Cumberland
to Wales by sea.

St. Herbert of Derwentwater

We do not know whether or not St. Kentigern stationed priests
in Cumberland to carry on the work he had begun, but we do
know that in the century after his death a holy man was living
on an island in Derwentwater not far from the place where
Kentigern is supposed to have set up his cross. St. Herbert's
Island—as it is still called—is one of the largest islands in Derwentwater and stands almost in the dead centre of the lake. It is wooded
now, and has the ruins of a chapel which may belong to the fourteenth century when the bishop ordered that the vicar of Crosthwaite should say Mass on the island once a year on St. Herbert's
Day (13th April). Priests, acolytes and country folk walked from
the parish church to the shores of the lake, rowed across the water,
and earned an indulgence of forty days for their attendance at
the festival.

From the island they could see some of the most magnificent
views of Cumberland. But St. Herbert did not choose his retreat
because its beauty appealed to him. He chose it, one may suppose,
for the very opposite reason, because it seemed to offer nothing
to attract the eye or distract the mind. We are told of St. Cuthbert
that on Lindisfarne he lived in a cell of which "the wall on the outside is higher than a man, but within, by excavating the rock,
he made it much deeper, to prevent the eyes and the thoughts
from wandering, that the mind might be wholly bent on heavenly
things, and the pious inhabitant might behold nothing from his
residence but the heavens above him."[2]

It seems very likely that Herbert shared this attitude to nature,
since he and Cuthbert were firm friends. We have it from the
Venerable Bede that when Cuthbert visited Carlisle, the hermit
of the lake went there to see him, and asked that he might be

---

[1] The first syllable of this name is probably derived from Mungo. See: *The
Place-Names of Cumberland* (Cambridge Univ. Press).
[2] Bede: *Life and Miracles of St. Cuthbert.* (*Everyman* translation.)

allowed to pray that they should meet death in the same hour.[1]

Indeed, the same attitude to wild nature persisted many centuries after St. Herbert. In 1759 John Wesley made one of his several visits to the colliers of Whitehaven and moved on to preach in the Vale of Lorton, near Cockermouth. And the people who came to hear him, he says, "found God to be a God both of the hills and valleys, and no where more present than in the mountains of Cumberland."[2] The remark has sometimes been taken to show that Wesley anticipated Wordsworth in Wordsworth's own country. In fact, he meant that Lorton was the last place on earth where anyone might expect to find God, and that it was singular evidence of His mercy that He *could* be found there.

St. Bega

Cuthbert and Herbert died in 687, by which time the Lakes had been absorbed into the diocese of Lindisfarne. Moreover, the Synod of Whitby had been held in 664, after which it is generally understood that the English rites superseded the Celtic in the north of England, and that the Celtic Church was pushed back across the Border. In Cumberland, however, it seems likely that the Church remained predominantly Celtic for a long time after this. The Irish saints were still remembered, especially along the coast. There are several dedications in this area to St. Brigid and her cousin St. Patrick, while Kirksanton, in the south of the county, commemorates one of the several Irish saints called Sanctan.[3] But our closest connection with the Irish Church lies in the third and most charming of our medieval legends of the Saints—the story of St. Bega.

Bega, according to the most colourful version, was an Irish princess who fled by sea to avoid a Norwegian suitor, and was caught in a storm off the Cumberland coast. She may have hoped to land at Whitehaven, but the storm was driving her straight towards the great double headland to the south of it. She called on God, vowing that if she were saved she would live a life of

[1] "They never met again, but their souls departed from their bodies at one and the same moment of time, and were joined together in a heavenly vision, and translated at the same time by angels to the heavenly kingdom." Bede: *Op. cit.*

[2] John Wesley: *Journal.*

[3] Santon below Wasdale, however, seems to derive its name merely from "sand". See *Place-Names of Cumberland.*

prayer beneath the cliffs which threatened to dash the boat to
pieces. The boat was cast ashore, perhaps in the small Fleswick
Bay between the two promontories, and she and her attendant
woman managed to crawl up the sandstone slabs and to find refuge in a cave or hut. She then went to the Lord of Egremont
and asked him to grant her a small plot of land on which she could
build a hermitage. He was scornful. He would give her, he said,
as much land as was covered by snow the next day and on Midsummer Day. To anyone who knows the Cumberland weather
this would seem a rash promise. The snow fell, right enough,
covering a three-mile stretch of ground around the headlands,
along the Pow Beck and as far as Whitehaven. All trace of the
nunnery has gone—if either nunnery or St. Bega herself ever
existed—but the priory of St. Bees later rose on the lands which
the snow chose for the Church.

The Monasteries

In the years which preceded the Norman Conquest ecclesiastical affairs were very confused in the north-west. People were
rarely sure to what bishop they owed allegiance, and even after
Henry I had created the new bishopric of Carlisle, the diocese
still remained disunited and poorly organized. The Church, in
fact, carried out its spiritual and civilizing work chiefly through
the monasteries, of which there were eight or nine larger houses,
mostly founded by Norman barons. The Augustinians (Austin
Canons or Black Friars) set up priories at Carlisle, Lanercost and
Cartmel; the Premonstratensians, at Shap; the Benedictines, at
St. Bees and Wetheral, both of these being cells of St. Mary's,
York. The Cistercians established an abbey at Holme Cultram,
and the Cistercian rule was also observed at Furness and its
daughter house of Calder, though these two were founded, in
the first place, by the Benedictines. In addition there were a number of smaller houses: a priory of Augustinian Canons, originally
founded as a hospital, at Conishead, near Ulverston; settlements
of friars at Carlisle, Penrith and Appleby; and hospitals at Bardsea
and elsewhere.

There were also two houses of Benedictine nuns—at Armathwaite, in the north of Cumberland, and at Seaton, near Bootle.
The Border, towards the end of the Middle Ages, was not the
safest place for communities of virgins, and Armathwaite seems

frequently to have been plundered, while at Seaton, though they escaped the raiders, the nuns were wretchedly poor. The annual income per head at Armathwaite has been estimated at about £2. 14. 0. as compared with over £24 per head for the monks of Furness,[1] and Seaton was almost certainly worse off than Armathwaite, for they had few endowments and could expect little help from the barren moorlands around Black Combe. Seaton, one suspects, was maintained less for the glory of God than as a home where minor landowners could farm out their unmarriageable daughters on payment of a small dowry.

Of the monasteries to the north and east of the area, Carlisle (or what was left of the church by the Reformers and Roundheads) is now the cathedral, Lanercost and Holme Cultram (the village is known as Abbeytown) have survived, in part, as parish churches, while Shap—the white limestone abbey by the banks of the River Lowther in Westmorland—is entirely in ruins.

Of the monasteries which carried out their work in the Lakes, some (such as Conishead) have more or less disappeared beneath farm buildings or post-reformation mansions. Others stand well-displayed as ruins, and some still play their part in the religious life of their district. Let us look at one or two examples of each.

Cartmel Priory

Cartmel was by no means the largest of the Lake District monasteries, but its church is undoubtedly our finest medieval building. It lies in a shallow dint of a valley that, instead of cutting back among the mountains, seems to push itself out as a peninsula between the estuaries of the Kent and the Leven. Cartmel was really the priory of the sands rather than of the hills, and many of the parishioners, who had their own chapel of St. Michael within the abbey church building, were fishermen and cocklers from Flookburgh and Allithwaite. This peninsula, jutting out into Morecambe Bay like the middle strokes of a capital "M", was the obvious halting-place on the cross-bay journey where travellers could wait, during the hours of high-tide, either at the village inns or in the priory itself. There is still an old mile-stone (or, rather, guide-stone) in the village which gives the distance to Lancaster and Ulverston by the over-sands route. In fact, the Prior and Canons of Cartmel were responsible for maintaining

[1] See: *The Lake Counties: 1500–1830*, C. M. L. Bouch and G. P. Jones.

a guide (usually called "The Carter") for the Kent Estuary, just as the monks of Conishead looked after the Leven.[1]

Cartmel village today is leisurely, ecclesiastic and not obviously on the road to anywhere. A tradesman, delivering in the district, is said to have passed within a hundred yards of the village once a week for years without discovering that it was there. Today, however, it gets many visitors, and is crowded every Whit Saturday and Monday for the annual race-meeting. The River Eea moons through it, between walls and behind bridges, at most times flowing scarcely fast enough to rock the water crow-foot. There is a tiny town square with shops, houses, inns and the old priory gatehouse, all cramped together, yet so disposed and ordered, that they might be a stage-set for an Edwardian musical comedy. The village is conscious of its beauty, yet without coyness or undue pride. The houses are there to be lived in rather than to be looked at. There are cats on the steps and apple trees bulging up like captive balloons behind the limestone walls.

In the winter, it is a grey village; in spring, it is starch-white against the burst and spikiness of back-garden green. But in autumn, limestone and leaves alike are mulled over with yellows and browns, and the village becomes a Harvest-Festival jumble of roofs, trees, gables and virginia creeper. Wordsworth's old teacher, William Taylor of Hawkshead Grammar School (the "Matthew" of the Matthew poems), is buried in the churchyard, and the lines from Gray, mentioned in *The Prelude*,[2] can still be read on his tombstone. My own great-grandfather farmed at Hard Crag, just outside the village, and my grandfather was married to my grandmother in the priory, where my grandmother, who could not write, put her mark in the register. Today Cartmel has a handsome modern secondary school, the central school for the district, and one of the few of its kind to be built by the Church of England during recent years.

The village no doubt owes its existence (and, today, a good deal of its livelihood) to the priory, and, in return, the priory owes its present existence to the villagers, but for whom it would have been let go to ruin at the Dissolution. For the Cartmel people

---

[1] According to tradition Mass was said for travellers on Chapel Island about a mile from the shore. This was the spot where Wordsworth heard the news of the death of Robespierre—*The Prelude*, Book X.

[2] *The Prelude* (1860). Book X; lines 531-52.

Coniston Water from the north

claimed the Chapel of St. Michael, in the south-east aisle of the choir—now called "The Town Choir"—and were allowed to continue worshipping there, while the chancel had its roof ripped off and was left to rot in the rain. Between 1618 and 1620, the the chancel was re-roofed, walls and windows were repaired, and a new carved screen and canopies were added to the fifteenth-century canons' stalls which had somehow survived beneath the rubble and rough weather of eighty years.

I do not intend to repeat the information given in pamphlets on sale in the church.[1] It is enough to say that this church compels our wonder less by the details of craftsmanship (much of the nave, in fact, is rather crudely built, like a barn, of undressed stone) than by its organic wholeness. I once began a poem about it:

"God's box of bricks . . ."

That was all I managed to write but it was all I needed. For seen from the ground, the church is a huge child's castle of cubes tipped half-over so that the under-half is hidden inside. The old late-thirteenth-century tower is a cube, hardly higher than the roofs of choir and transepts. And the fifteenth-century tower (added about the same time as the Perpendicular east window) is another cube, half the size of the old one, and set diagonally inside it. The odd, one-box-inside-the-other effect of this double tower was not likely to start a new architectural fashion, but it gives to the building an individuality as strong as the local dialect; so that the whole church is like an enormous houseleek of gables, windows, battlements, buttresses, angles and wall-ends.

Inside, the crossing has a spaciousness not always achieved in larger buildings. There are the round, dog-toothed arches of the choir, with the triforium arcade above them, all in the rich, shortbread-coloured stone. But things like these, beautiful as they are, can be seen in other churches. What makes Cartmel specially memorable is its woodwork. The old canons' stalls, with their carved misericords, are full of humour and imaginative conceits—birds, beasts, devils, an angel and a mermaid. And set upon the old bases are the canopies, which, together with the screen, were given to the priory by George Preston of Holker Hall and inserted

[1] *A New Guide to Cartmel Priory Church* by J. C. Dickinson, a noted historian of medieval monasticism. See also: *Cartmel, People and Priory* by Sam Taylor (Titus Wilson, Kendal).

Grasmere lake and village and slopes of Seat Sandal

about 1620. These are quite different from the kind of woodwork
we usually see in old English churches—the predominantly
"architectural" style of most medieval canopies (as, for instance,
in Carlisle Cathedral) or the exuberant cornucopias of Grinling
Gibbons. Instead, there is a row of Corinthian columns with a
screen of pierced panels behind them, continually varying in
pattern, while the columns are entwined with vines and decorated
with emblems of the Passion—hammer, pincers, whip and so
on. The total effect of the work is elegant, almost sophisticated,
and yet, in this black wood, above the weather-worn and time-
worn bench-ends and the grotesque heads of the misericords, it
is also deeply moving. In a land where nature beats man nine
hundred and ninety-nine times out of a thousand in the production
of beauty, this is one of the few things worth going indoors to
see.

St. Bees

The old Benedictine priory of St. Bees has adapted itself to
modern life in a rather different way. It was founded in the reign
of Henry I on what may have been the site of St. Bega's hermitage
or nunnery, and, as with Holme Cultram, most of it was destroyed
at the Reformation. What is left—i.e. the abbey church except
for the choir, which was blocked off and allowed to go to ruin—
has now become the parish church to the village.

I must not say much about the building itself, or these pages will
be filled with architectural description. In any case St. Bees, unlike
Cartmel, is not a tourist attraction—parties do not come there by
coach for the Sunday morning service. Yet it is one of the most
interesting churches in Cumberland, with a particularly fine west
end, made up of a Norman doorway, three Early English lights,
and a single gable window above. The stone itself is exceptionally
beautiful—a deep, red sandstone, red as cochineal. It is soft, too,
so that the angular decorations of the doorway are being rubbed
away as the face of the stone is re-carved by the weather into the
smooth organic shapes of bones and shells. It looks so soft that
you feel you could mould and shape it with your fingers. The rain
soaks into it, and in wet weather it grows as brown as coffee, and
everywhere, on church, graveyard walls, and the old houses
round about, there is a bright green weed with a minute white
flower. Botanists who wish to know what it is must wait for the

publication of the new official *Flora of Cumberland* now in preparation by Dr. Derek Radcliffe.

When the church was restored by Butterworth during the nineteenth century the tower was given a new belfry with a low, slated steeple like those of the small towers of Southwell Cathedral. To my mind this was well suited to a Norman building and fitted in with the landscape. But in more recent years slates began to work loose, causing damage and incurring the cost of repeated repairs, so that it was decided to heighten the walls of the tower, thus boxing in and half-hiding the little steeple. Visitors to the churchyard are now no longer in danger of having their heads sliced off as they bend to examine the dusky cranesbill that grows there, but the church has lost its French accent. It is good to be able to say that the new stone, which at first looked as pink as tinned salmon, is rapidly weathering to the shade of the older walls.

In 1817, a theological college was established at St. Bees, to house which the old choir of the church was roofed and restored. The college came to an end in the 1890s, and the hall—a reconstruction of some very attractive Transitional work—is used for various parochial purposes.

But this is not all that has happened to the old priory. Edmund Grindall, who succeeded Matthew Parker in 1575 as Archbishop of Canterbury, was born somewhere in the district (possibly at Hensingham) and almost certainly attended the priory school, which, of course, was closed after the Dissolution. Realizing how much it would be missed, he persuaded Queen Elizabeth to grant Letters Patent to found a free grammar school at St. Bees. It was one of the last acts of his life, and he did not live to see the setting up of the school. Indeed, the gap in time between priory school and public school was so great that the latter was not able to take over any of the old buildings, though no doubt many of the stones from the old house went to the making of the new one, as they did, also, into nearby farms, one of which is still called The Abbey.

The quadrangle, with one Elizabethan wing, faces the twisting main road and is rather pinched in appearance, but the school spreads sideways, as if it were advertising itself to the railway line. Most of the buildings are of the same sandstone as the priory, dug from the huge blackberry-coloured quarries near the village, but the new Memorial Hall, above the playing field, is of wood and glass, with Josephine de Vasconcellos's *Hand of God*[1] in Honister slate standing close beside it.

Generations of parsons' sons and the sons of professional men have been educated there, and, though it draws many of its pupils from a wider area, it remains essentially the public school of Cumberland. It is not for one who did not go there to speak of its achievements or traditions, but even to an outsider it must be evident that such an environment—the old priory, the dour little village, the wild coast and the fells not far away—must have had a lasting effect on many a sensitive youth. Today, as might be expected, St. Bees is no longer isolated. The little, red-paved bay beneath the cliffs is now a bathing parade for the girls of Whitehaven, which may have a different effect on a sensitive youth, and the village itself is in danger of being turned into an outer suburb of the larger town.

The shore, which used to be perhaps the most attractive in Cumberland, has already been seriously spoiled. The high tides, rushing into the bottle-neck of the cove, had damaged the shingle bank, so that it was necessary to strengthen it, but this has been taken as an excuse to make a promenade with seats, steps, concrete slopes and a vast car park. Anyone who wants to see St. Bees as it used to be had better climb the not-too-steep path along the edge of the cliffs, until he can look into Fleswick Bay and on the guillemots and kittiwakes nesting on the rocks near the lighthouse.

Furness Abbey

The monks of the north-west chose to build nearly all their larger houses on sandstone—Cartmel and Shap being the two notable exceptions—and Furness Abbey is on one of the very few outcrops of this rock to be found in North Lonsdale.

The soil of the Vale of the Deadly Nightshade[2] is dark and rich; there are escarpments of red rock, and the trees hang down the slopes, fat and heavy. After the cheerful limestone of the Dalton district, the dark red walls seem sullen and introspective, greened over with moss and mould.

When the abbey was founded in 1127, through the gift of

[1] One of the largest works of sculpture yet carried out in slate.
[2] The flower still grows among the ruins.

Stephen, afterwards King of England, Furness was a wild, isolated part of the country, inhabited by a rough people, speaking a dialect still half-Norse. But the abbey prospered, and at one time its possessions were almost as extensive as the Isle of Man. It owned farms and woodland, with their wool-trade and hunting rights, together with fishing rights in the Morecambe Bay estuaries and on Windermere and Coniston Water. It owned mills, salt-pans, and numerous small iron-ore mines, and the monks ran a considerable export and smuggling trade from Piel Harbour. It was on Piel that the half-witted Lambert Simnel landed in 1487, with a large body of Irish and Flemish soldiers, to claim the throne of Henry VII. The Abbot of Furness kept aloof from this rising, but in 1536 the monks had a certain amount of rather ambiguous dealings with the leaders of The Pilgrimage of Grace—enough, at any rate, to give the king's commissioners an excuse for dissolving the community and pulling down the buildings.

Had Barrow-in-Furness then been in existence, even as a sizeable village, the church might have been spared as were the churches at St. Bees and Cartmel. But it was judged that the parish church of Dalton was all that was needed to serve the few people on this tip of the peninsula, and the abbey was tumbled into ruin. Today it finds itself almost enclosed within the suburbs of a large industrial town, yet it is still astonishingly secluded, hidden away in a deep trough behind a huge rampart of trees.[1] Recently the ruins have been the setting for the Furness Mystery Plays, selected from the cycles of York, Chester and Wakefield, and performed by local actors during the month of July, and it is hoped that these may be repeated every three years.

Because of its nearness to the town it is not surprising that the abbey grounds look rather like a municipal park. The lawns are cut and the paths are weeded. Moreover, the Ministry of Works has taken charge of the ruins, and torn down ivy and tree, propped up the walls with bolt and bar, and pumped cement into the cracks among the stones. What four hundred years of weather

---

[1] ". . . To more than inland peace,
Left by the west wind sweeping overhead
From a tumultuous ocean, trees and towers
In that sequestered valley may be seen,
Both silent and both motionless alike."
Wordsworth: *The Prelude* (1860). Book II; lines 108–12.

has left standing is to be preserved, as far as possible, for the next four hundred years. And all this was rightly done, for Furness is a text-book abbey, a large-scale model for the student, almost complete in the details of its foundation plan—church, chapter-house, cloisters, dormitories, infirmary, kitchen, abbot's lodging and even the drainage and sewage system. Its grandeur does not depend on the romantic associations of change and decay. It is massive, bare and austere, with a long nave, and with the chancel arch still intact, high and poised. The sedilia in the chancel wall have an elaborately-carved stone canopy, and the chapter house, too, was fairly richly ornamented. The bases of the six pillars still stand there, after the manner of classic ruins, and, though the roof is entirely gone, you can see by looking at the roof of the in-firmary chapel how beautiful it must have been, ribbed and curv-ing like bats' wings. Apart from these, and the pillars and arches of the cloisters, there is little decoration. Most of the stone is as plain as when it was quarried. Yet nothing is lacking, for this abbey does not need ornament, just as it does not need legends or ghosts or the ivy and trailing ferns which the Ministry of Works has torn away. It was never a mere assemblage of artistic felicities. Its greatness lay in the way every stone was dedicated and adapted to the purpose for which it was intended. It was, in fact, as func-tional in design as a blast furnace.

Calder Abbey

The River Calder runs along one of the smaller valleys which make up the western segment of Wordsworth's cartwheel. It rises very near Ennerdale, but flows south-west, receiving the becks which come from the Haycock, Steeple and Pillar group. The country is desolate, shapeless and monotone. Then, a few miles above the abbey, the river cuts into the St. Bees sandstone. There is no instant change in the landscape, but the river flows in deep ravines, and you can see the red buttresses and slabs under the water, with grey and blue cobbles at the water's edge, washed down from the upper fells. The river now slices down into its narrow valley where trees bubble up to meet it and farms and walls are all of sandstone. Below Sella Park the land flattens, and the river frays out into a pebbly delta with willows growing on little islands in mid-stream. The runnels unite again and flow under the railway on to the sands, where the channel of the Calder meets that of the Ehen, coming from Ennerdale, so that at low tide it might almost be regarded as a tributary of the longer stream.

Thirty years ago this spot was one of the loneliest on the Cumberland coast. Today it is the site of Windscale and Calder Hall— the first atomic power station in the world. No one with more imagination than a hen will pretend that Windscale is likely to make the future more comfortable for Cumberland, but when the two filter towers first went up they had a tall, unearthly, sinister elegance which emphasized, rather than destroyed, the bareness of the coast. Since then a number of industrial cooling-towers have been added to the site, taking away much of its individuality. Yet in the blue-hazy days of late autumn the steam from the towers gives a romantic wash to the coast-scape as seen, for instance, from Bootle shore, with the guns of Eskmeals firing tracer-shells over the full tide. And there is one spot from the Birker Moor road, as it descends into Eskdale by Red Gill, where you can see the towers, like an uneven bottom set of false teeth, clamped in the jaws of the gill. The distant, inhuman, cataclysmic past of the granite is brought right against the perhaps not very different future of the atom.

By one of the ironies of topography there are only about two miles of river-flow between Calder Abbey and Calder Hall. The abbey was founded in 1134 by a colony of monks and lay-brothers from Furness, who, however, fled before the coming of William FitzDuncan and the Scots, leaving their wooden church to be burnt. (They then went on to Bylands in Yorkshire.) Later the Abbot of Furness sent out another batch of monks, and the building of the abbey proceeded until the fourteenth century with, apparently, little interruption from Scottish raiders. The local tradition saying that the abbey was partially destroyed in the Scottish raid of 1322 has not been confirmed by archaeological examination of the ruins. Indeed, the worst destruction seems to have come from post-Dissolution owners, one of whom drove a road through the chancel, while another built cow-sheds in the gate-house and the south transepts.[1] When Thomas Rymer bought the estate in the late nineteenth century, loads of stones from the abbey were being carted away for building walls, and it was only the prompt action of the new owner which saved the ruins from

[1] I am indebted to the late Miss M. C. Fair for this information.

almost total obliteration. During the last war the ruins became badly overgrown, but this has now been put right, and the owners continue to take great care of their stupendous heritage. It is, nevertheless, a very great responsibility for any private person, however conscientious, and one cannot but wonder—even at the risk of giving offence—whether a monument of such importance should not be in the care of a public body.

The remains, in any case, are not nearly so extensive as those at Furness. The west wall, with a Norman doorway, dates from the twelfth century. The nave was built in the next century, and one aisle remains, leading to the tower over the high and graceful chancel arch. The north transept has a particularly lovely Early English doorway, while the chapter house has remains of a decorated window and one bay of a three-bay groined roof. The juxtaposition of styles, stepping up through the centuries, has a special charm, yet the chief appeal of Calder is not architectural, but, as it were, literary. It might have been the setting for a ballad by Scott or a novel by Anne Radcliffe—who, in fact, visited the abbeys of Furness and Shap, though she did not reach Calder. It is, in any case, a place for assignations, murders and ghosts, and it is told that a monk occasionally appears in photographs, looking out of one of the windows of the mansion built over the abbey foundations. During the war, when the ruins were overhung with ivy and blackberry, they looked like a Victorian vignette. Even today they remain secluded, secret, unready to give explanations. The historian will find more to interest him at Furness, but, for the unashamed romantic, Calder gives the fancy one extra turn.

The Parish Churches

In Cumberland and Westmorland there is no local tradition in church architecture such as we find in the Cotswolds or East Anglia. For one thing, the dales were mostly too poor. For another, the slate was not a good material, or not, at least, for building in the styles of the medieval gothic. Moreover, partly because of the poverty and partly because of the slate, churches fell into disrepair and had to be rebuilt, or they proved to be too small and had to be enlarged. So that while we have many dale churches of twelfth or thirteenth century foundation, only a few of them remain in anything like their original state.

The finest of our largest churches stand outside the dales. It is not my aim to give a list of all those which are worth a visit. There are many—I am glad to say—which I myself have not yet visited, for I will sometimes pass a church a score of times before I make up my mind to stop and go inside and it will be sad for me when I feel that there is none left to discover. But out of some thirty years' persistent, desultory and unsystematic stopping and popping in, certain buildings stay in the memory. On the edge of the area, the Eden Valley holds the churches of Appleby and Kirkby Stephen, while the Lune holds Sedbergh and Kirkby Lonsdale. At Sedbergh the children still tie up the churchyard gate during weddings and will not let the bride and bridegroom come through until they have paid a ransom in scattered coppers. Nearer the Lakes, but again not really in the dales, is Greystoke, between Keswick and Penrith, a collegiate church, and one of the most attractive in the diocese, which owes much to the benefactions of the Huddlestons—a branch of the family which produced the author[1] of *Naught for Your Comfort*. The same family gave to Holy Trinity, Millom, a fourteenth-century chapel (really, a south aisle to the nave) which is one of the most serenely beautiful inventions of man to be found in these parts. A particular curve is repeated and varied, as if musically, in the tracery of the windows, one of which, "the fish window", a gothic arch reflected upside-down beneath itself, is unequalled of its kind in England.

I let my memory move across the Duddon into the district once in the care of the monks of Furness, where the church at Urswick, founded before the abbey, still stands beside a tarn which has always been called "bottomless". Some of the Saxon work still remains, but it is not that which I remember, but the fancies of an early nineteenth-century wood-carver, who has decorated the choir stalls and the organ with all manner of musical instruments—viols, pipes and drums, even a barrel-organ with its monkey. Not far away, at Aldingham, is the church which became specially associated with the Durham miners from their convalescent home at Conishead Priory. Aldingham has a leper's squint—and, indeed, the whole church has something of a squint, since of the two arcades which run down the nave, one is of round arches, the other of pointed. It stands right on the kerb of More-

[1] The Rt. Rev. Trevor Huddleston

cambe Bay, with a wreckage of cobbles around it and the spring
tides battering at the churchyard wall.

Across the bay are the churches of the limestone district of the
Kent estuary, over which the five-aisled parish church of Kendal
(i.e. having a nave and two aisles on either side) broods like a hen
gathering her chickens under her wing. Some of the chickens
got away, however, and grew up by themselves—the parish
churches of Burton-in-Kendal, Heversham, Beetham and the
rest. At first glance, Beetham has the kind of prettiness which
you expect on a coloured calendar, with the river running close
by, and an avenue of rambler roses from gate to porch. Inside,
it has a graver beauty. My grandmother was baptized here—
her father being a gamekeeper on the Dallam Tower estate.

Memory nags me into listing a few more even at the risk of
growing tedious: Isel, on the River Derwent, where the narrow
windows and thick walls remind us of the Border raids, for,
though it may not have been used as a place of refuge, as the
church of Great Salkeld undoubtedly was, it was none the less
built to withstand fire; Hawkshead, Wordsworth's "snow-white
church upon the hill"; Bowness-on-Windermere, surrounded
by a great grave-yard of parked cars; Grasmere; Crosthwaite;
and St. Bridget's, Beckermet, a lost-looking church, almost
equally maltreated by restoration and neglect, which by now must
be almost radio-active.

The Dale Churches

Yet none of these is quite a church of the dales, for the dale
churches are usually smaller, plainer, sometimes rather mean in
furniture and trappings, but often with a gruff bareness that
knocks at the heart like poverty. Most of them have the look of
a barn, with no decoration at all on the outside except, perhaps,
for a little freestone tracery in the windows. Many have served
a community of the same dozen or score of families for generation
after generation, perhaps under the care of a parson who was himself part-time spinner and weaver and part-time farmer, if not,
sometimes, almost part-time beggar.

Four such churches come into my mind, in widely separated
parts, all of which have the reek of antiquity in their bones.
There is St. Anthony, Cartmel Fell, in the valley of the Winster,
so low that it seems almost entrenched in its own grave-yard

Inside, the smell and aura of the past is so strong that it might have been canned like fruit. There are two beautifully-carved pews, a three-decker pulpit, and some fifteenth-century glass [1] depicting, among other things, St. Anthony and his pig. Cartmel Fell is now much visited, and so, too, is the old church at Martindale, on the east side of Ullswater, though it has to be approached by a switchback of a road from Howtown. For ordinary parochial purposes this church has been superseded by the larger, nineteenth-century building on the hill, but it is neat and cared-for and gives a good idea of what the dale churches must have been like in the century or so after the Reformation. It stands at the entrance to Bannerdale which—together with the parallel Boredale—is about the most deserted hidden-away valley still left in the Lakes.

Mungrisdale, a church very similar in outward appearance, still serves its parish, and lies only two miles north of the main Keswick–Penrith road, close to Souther Fell, the scene of the phantom procession which seemed to foretell the Rebellion of the '45. It contains a wall-tablet to the memory of Raisley Calvert, father of the young man of the same name who was nursed by Wordsworth, and left the poet the small legacy which helped him to set up house with Dorothy at Grasmere.

My fourth church is the least visited of them all—at Hall Waberthwaite, about a mile off the Whitehaven–Millom road, north of Bootle. This hamlet of a few farms and cottages—the hall itself has fallen down—stands where the rough road peters out on the banks of the River Esk near a ford leading to the steep wood-slopes of Muncaster. At this point the Esk scarcely knows whether it is still a river or already an inlet of the sea. The estuary is no wider than a decent-sized pond, and you cannot get even the most distant glimpse of the sea, but the marshes smell of salt, while sea asters and sea lavender bloom in mourning colours in the mud, and the high tide fills the gullies to the brim. Like so many of the dale churches this is a plain rectangle in form. There are rough, old-fashioned box-pews, but it has little of the consciously archaic about it. You feel that it has not yet accustomed itself to receiving extra-parochial visitors. Its antiquity is

[1] It has been suggested that the glass came from Cartmel Priory, but the figure of St. Anthony, the patron saint, must surely have been made for the church of his name.

irrelevant and it goes on with its job with the persistence of a farmer who still uses the horse-plough to turn a field which the tractors cannot tackle. In spring the crocuses are so thick in the graveyard that you cannot walk along the path without treading on them. (The sandy soil of this part of the coastal strip seems particularly favourable to crocuses, and also to primroses which mass on the slopes of the railway cuttings in acres at a time. The cowslip, however, is almost unknown.)

This air of belonging to no particular age or time is characteristic, too, of the chapels of the high dales. Some of them, in fact, are not particularly old, and many have been ruthlessly restored or rebuilt. Some are rough-cast and perhaps whitewashed; while in others the slate is left uncovered as in a byre. The most famous are probably those at Buttermere—so perfect that it might have been built for a film set—at Mardale and at Wasdale. The old church at Mardale, of course, is now under the waters of Haweswater reservoir, but that at Wasdale Head still stands, surrounded by the graves of fallen climbers in what are perhaps the flattest acres of dry land in the whole of Cumberland. From, say, a few hundred yards up the track to Black Sail Pass, this tract is seen to be scored and parcelled out by the stone walls into dozens of irregular four and more sided figures, of which that belonging to the church looks no different from the rest except for its yews.

Compared to the church of the upper dale that of the middale is often rather larger, as is the case at the very interesting Strands, in Wasdale, and again at St. John the Baptist, Ulpha, in the Duddon Valley. Ulpha still has oil lamps and fragments of eighteenth-century black and white paintings on the walls, and in the graveyard there is a stone to the memory of a Whitehaven man "who perished on Birker Moor during the pelting of the pitiless storm on the 1st of January 1826". The chapel of Seathwaite, three miles higher up the same dale, must have been altogether homelier and more cottage-like in the days of its most famous curate, Wonderful Walker,[1] but it was almost entirely rebuilt—and, as one might say, *ecclesiastified*—during the last

---

[1] The Revd. Robert Walker (1709–1802). The best account of this now almost legendary figure is to be found in Wordsworth's notes on *The River Duddon: A series of Sonnets*. Wordsworth's description of the descent into Dunnerdale from Walna Scar by Long House Gill is still substantially accurate and superbly perceptive.

century, and the interior, though still pleasing, has lost its former starkness. Outside, however, it remains plain slate, which means that it looks as if it belongs where it is. This is true of all the dale churches, old or new—Coniston, Torver, Woodland, Great Langdale, Kentmere, Matterdale, Patterdale or "Wythburn's modest house of prayer". Few of them are notable works of architecture, some have hardly a stone which is earlier than the reign of Victoria, but nearly all are as home-bred as the Herdwick sheep. They have the merit, also, of being—almost all of them— low-built, for slate is no material for steeples and steeples are hopelessly out of place among the fells. Where nineteenth-century builders have imported materials and set up steeples—as, for instance, at Ambleside and St. John's, Keswick—the result looks insignificant. In fact, the only steeples in the Lake country which are really effective are those set on detached hills in the lower-lying outer lands—All Saints', Cockermouth, or St. George's, Millom, where the spire spikes up against the western sky when seen from almost any point on the Duddon Sands.

The Quakers

Another religious body has contributed to the Lake scene buildings which rival the dale churches in their bare severity. The Quakers, indeed, have played an important part in the development of Cumberland and Westmorland—especially in the industrial towns outside the mining area. According to Burn and Nicolson, they first appeared in the district at Kirkby Stephen, where the vicar, Francis Higginson, incited the magistrates against them in the time of Oliver Cromwell.[1]

It seems extremely unlikely that these Solomon-Eagle-like revivalists were indeed followers of George Fox, but the incident

---

[1] "Mr. Higginson produceth instances of these people running about the streets, foaming and bellowing out such like expressions as these: 'Repent, repent! Wo, wo! The Judge of the world is come!' Some of them stood naked upon the market cross, on the market days, preaching from thence to the people. Particularly, he mentions the wife of one Edmund Adlington, of Kendal, who went naked through the streets there; and two others of the Society, a man and a woman, who called themselves Adam and Eve, went publicly naked, and when questioned concerning the same at the assizes, the man affirmed that the power of God was upon him, and he was commanded so to do."
The History and Antiquities of the Counties of Westmorland and Cumberland, J. Nicolson and R. Burn (1777).

shows that the people of the Westmorland–Yorkshire Pennines were ready to listen to the unorthodox preacher. So that when Fox came to Sedbergh in 1652, passing on to Firbank where he preached a famous sermon on the stone outside the chapel, his words fell on fruitful ground. Some of his best-known followers came from the land between the Lune and the Kent, including Francis Howgill and Edward Burrough, the "Son of Thunder and Consolation". The following year Fox came to Cumberland. He went first to Bootle, on the coast, where he was set on by a band of toughs, and moved on through Cockermouth and Caldbeck to Carlisle, where he was imprisoned "in the dungeon among the moss-troopers, thieves and murderers".[1]

About a hundred and twenty years later, in 1772, an American Quaker, John Woolman, feeling "a religious concern to visit Friends in the northern parts of England", made a kind of pilgrimage in the steps of George Fox. He visited Kendal, Preston Patrick and York (where he died of the smallpox), writing on the way a journal which has taken its place among the literary heritage of the American people. Woolman must have looked even odder than his forerunner of the leather breeches, for he went about entirely in un-dyed cloth, refusing to have anything to do with the vegetable dyes which were produced by slave labour.

Yet Woolman did not visit Swarthmoor near Ulverston, which has perhaps stronger ties with Fox than any other spot in the Lakes. For at Swarthmoor Hall he was sheltered by Judge Fell, whose widow, Margaret Fell, he later married. Near Swarthmoor there is a seventeenth-century Quaker meeting-house of grave, grey beauty, outside and inside, and with its own small burial ground. Fox's widow (who has been called the Mother of Quakerism) was not buried here, however, but a few miles away in the Friends' burial ground at Sunbrick on Birkrigg Common. There was another burial ground in the Duddon Valley roughly opposite "The Traveller's Rest" which may have been used by

---

[1] George Fox: *Journal.*

He goes on: "A filthy, nasty place it was, where men and women were put together in a very uncivil manner, and never a house of office to it; and the prisoners so lousy that one woman was almost eaten to death by lice. Yet, bad as the place was, the prisoners were all made very loving and subject to me; and some of them were convinced of the truth, as the publicans and harlots were of old."

the inhabitants of Woodend, an isolated settlement with a Quaker meeting-house near Devoke Water.

Most of the other nonconformist churches of the district are of the nineteenth century, but the Baptist Church at Tottlebank, near Penny Bridge in the Crake Valley, belongs to the seventeenth, and is, in fact, one of the oldest of that denomination in the North of England. It stands a hundred yards or so from the road, looking indistinguishable, at that distance, from a farm. Its first minister was Gabriel Camelford, who had been the presbyterian vicar of Staveley during the Commonwealth. On his ejection by the Act of Uniformity in 1662 he allied himself with the Anabaptists and went to Tottlebank, making it a centre for the Puritan sympathizers of Low Furness, including the important Sawrey family of Broughton Towers, who almost alone among the local gentry, had supported Cromwell during the Civil War.

VII

THE MARK OF MAN—
FARMS, FORESTS AND RESERVOIRS

MONOLITHS, stone circles, forts, crosses, castles, abbeys, churches are the main memorials of man, but they are not the main mark which he has left on the district. For the landscape of the Lakes is a living thing, changing and evolving all the time. At the bottom the shape of the land is the shape of the rock, but the surface covering of that shape is largely what man has chosen to give it in his daily life and work. It was not, primarily, the Romans building their Wall, or the barons, their castles, or the monks, their monasteries who helped to make the landscape of Cumberland and Westmorland, but the men with the axe and the plough, the sheep-farmers, the quarrymen and the miners. And, oddly enough, the men who made the greatest mark of all were among the earliest of our settlers.

The Felling of the Forests

When the ice retreated from the fells it was probably sedges and mosses which colonized the land, then the alpine flowers, and then the trees. First there would be dwarf willows and birches and then the silver birch which is still the characteristic tree of the dales. Borrowdale is famous for them, and it gives its name to such places as Birker Moor, Birkrigg and Birks Bridge. It is at its happiest beside a garrulous dale beck as it climbs up and down the banks and leans over the rocks, getting its food from among the boulders. It is not a tree which you notice much at a distance, yet often, when you come across it suddenly, the whole dip of the valley seems just a V-shaped frame for the tree as it riddles the sky through its leaves.

Yet it was not the birch but the oak which became the dominant tree. By the time the Ice Age had entirely given way to the present temperate climate,[1] the "climax" vegetation of the dales was a

[1] There have been recurring periods, since the Ice Age, in which the climate was somewhat warmer than it is at present, possibly including the period when the Norsemen first colonized the dales.

Sheep farm below Place Fell, near Patterdale

thick oak scrub, mixed with chestnuts and some other deciduous trees, which filled the valley bottoms and climbed to a considerable height on the fellsides. The first men in the Lakes lived above the tree-line on what are now bleak moors. But as the hunter gave way to the agriculturist, and as flint scrapers gave way to axes which would cut wood, men began to fell the trees.

No doubt the process was very slow. Medieval Cumberland still had three great forests—Inglewood and Allerdale in the north, and Copeland around Ennerdale and Wasdale—and, though the term "forest" meant not necessarily woodland but land enclosed for the protection of game, Inglewood, at least, was well wooded and famous for its timber. In the Lakes proper, an early result of the felling of the woods was that the dale-bottoms became habitable and soon proved to be fertile. After all, "thwaite", a clearing, is about the commonest of all elements in our place-names.

But the success of settlement in the dales led to further felling which brought about a further result. For the land lost its annual supply of leaf-mould, it lost protection from wind and frost, and, above all, it lost the reinforcement of tree-roots which had bound and knitted the soil together. The valley-sides and the lower fell-slopes were exposed to sun, wind, frost, rain and the scouring of the sykes and becks. And then, as if to speed up this process of erosion, the dalesmen took up sheep-farming.

Sheep

The native sheep of the dales is, of course, the Herdwick. I say "native" somewhat cautiously, for though there is no truth in the local legend that the breed first came ashore from a wrecked ship of the Armada, there does seem just a slight possibility that it may have been brought to Cumberland by the Vikings. More probably, it was evolved by them out of an indigenous breed which they found in the dales when they first arrived.

No animals look so much at home on the fells as do the Herdwicks, not even the fell ponies. They are small sheep with rather grizzled faces—lithe and hardy, able to climb like goats and leap over any but the highest wall. They are lean about the legs and flanks, though the wool which covers them like upholstery often hides this. It is only when they are allowed to laze about and fatten in the river-side meadows that they put on flesh and give the sweet mutton they are famous for. In the past, much ewe-milk

Stone walls and snowdrift

cheese was eaten in the dales and hams of mutton were cured like bacon. When the sheep have been clipped in summer they look naked and white, but usually their wool is long and grey, with bits of dead bracken and thistle and dung stuck to it.

It is hard to think of the Herdwicks as domestic animals. They seem to belong to the land rather than to the farmer. The flock is often rented with the farm, and when the tenant leaves he has to make up any deficiency in the numbers and may take the benefit of any increase. Each flock has its own "heaf" or pasture on the fells where it spends the summer and autumn, and the sheep often know their own heaf so well that they will return to it from a long distance. Yet some of them stray, mingle with flocks not their own, so that, by a long tradition, the farmers meet twice a year to exchange foundlings and stragglers. Today strayed sheep are often returned by being bundled into the back of a farm van. But the Shepherds' Meet continues to be one of the great days of the dale year.

All sheep look very much alike and identification is made possible by an elaborate system of markings. First the sheep are smitten on the body with red ruddle or with tar,[1] or sometimes with blue or green staining. The marks are usually in the form of stripes, pops (i.e. round blobs) or letters, and are placed on different parts of the body. In addition—though this practice is now dying out—the ears are cut or marked in some distinctive way, or, sometimes, the horns are burned. Each farm inherits its own lug-marks which may go back far in history. The ears may be "cropped" (i.e. the end of the ear is chopped clean off), or "forked", or "ritted" (slit). They may be "fork-bitted" (i.e. a V-shaped notch is cut out of the side of the ear), or "key-bitted" (a square notch). And as there is a top and a bottom side to every ear with two ears to every sheep, the number of possible permutations and combinations is very great.

In 1817 J. Walker of Martindale compiled *The Shepherds Book*, which catalogued the lug-marks and smits belonging to the fell-farms west of the Eden. Several revisions were made and books brought out to cover other parts of the district, and I have beside me one of the most comprehensive of these volumes, Gates's *New*

---

[1] In the west coast district the ruddle usually came from small veins of haematite ore, the discovery of which in some cases led to the opening-up of the early iron mines.

Shepherd's Guide, published by The West Cumberland Times in 1879. This has nearly five hundred pages, with an engraving of the same two prize sheep repeated three times a page. On each engraving the smits are stamped in black and red, while the lugmarks are indicated diagrammatically, and there is added a technical description of the marks and the name of the farm and farmer to whom each belongs.

I open at the pages given to the parish of Whitbeck beside Black Combe:

John Grice, Far End:
cropped near, upper halved
far, stroke down near lisk,
pop on tailhead.

William Thompson, Barfield;
cropped and ritted near,
stroke from shoulder blade
on near side over back,
and to lisk on far side.

James Robinson, Hall Foss;
cropped near, ritted far, three red
strokes down far shoulder in the form
of a crow's foot, J. R. on near side.

George Kirkby, Beckside:
cropped and under key-bitted near,
under halved far, three short
strokes over back.

The practice of cutting the ears is now giving way to the use of metal identification tags or studs, though some of the more old-fashioned farmers still hang on to their lug-marks. I can hardly think that the change has been greatly regretted by the sheep.

But another practice which survived until about the beginning of this century must have worried them much less. This was the habit of counting the flocks in a set of Celtic numerals which had come down from the British tribes of pre-Viking Cumbria. The numbers are grouped in twenties so that when a shepherd had counted to a score he put a finger up and started again. When all five fingers were up he had reached the hundred, whereupon he put a pebble in his pocket or scratched a mark on a wall. The numerals vary a little in different parts of the district, but here is a version[1] gathered in the south of Cumberland:

"Yan, taen, tether, mether, pimp;
Teezar, leezar, catterah, horna, dick;
Yan-dick, tan-dick, tether-dick, mether-dick, bumpit;
Yan-a-bumpit, tan-bumpit, tedera-bumpit, medera-bumpit, gigot."

Sheep-farming, in fact, is so much the dominant industry of the dales that it has coloured the dalesman's language, his pastimes (the popularity of fell-hunting is due in good part to the need to protect the lambs), and even the way he builds his farms and cottages. Many of the latter, for instance, have "spinning-galleries" where the wool could hang out to dry in various stages of home spinning and weaving—a very good example can be seen at the farm just beyond High Yewdale Bridge on the Coniston–Ambleside main road and another outside "The Fisherman's Arms" at Spark Bridge. Again, during the wool boom of the sixteenth and seventeenth centuries, it was the Herdwick which began the prosperity of towns like Kendal, Ambleside and Hawkshead.

We have good reason, therefore, to be grateful to the sheep, but can surely find a better way of showing it than by slaughtering them at the road-sides. Yet this is what some of the visitors are doing by feeding them with picnic scraps. It is not just that cake and cucumber-sandwiches are not the best food for sheep, but that they are beginning to flock around the more popular picnic spots on the open fell-roads, such as the summit of Dunmail Raise, where they are likely to be run over by motorists and may cause serious accidents. They wander on to the road-sides and even sleep slap on the crown of the road, where, in mist or darkness it is very hard for a car-driver to spot them. In Scotland I have seen sheep climb up the steps of a bus to beg food from the passengers, but, until recently, I thought Cumbrian Herdwicks would have more sense.

Of course, it is possible that the sheep-feeding visitors are ecologists who are trying to re-adjust the balance of nature. For,

[1] Quoted from: *Millom People and Places*, Frank Warriner (Millom), 1937.

as far as the landscape is concerned, sheep-farming has been almost as destructive as the Ice Age. Sheep crop very closely, laying bare the surface to all the agents of erosion. And what is worse, they extract the minerals from the soil, transferring them into the wool instead of repaying them in the form of manure as the other animals do. The result of centuries of such impoverishment and erosion is that land which once could nourish oaks is now good for nothing but bracken.

Many people, of course, think of bracken as part of the "natural" scene in the Lakes in contrast to the "unnatural" changes and modifications brought about by man. In fact, the spread of bracken is due almost entirely to man. The old dale small-holder, struggling to scratch a living from two or three upland fields and a few acres of fell-pasture, had to scythe and dig and burn to get full use from every square yard of his land. The farmer of today simply cannot afford labour for this sort of work. So, since the time of Wordsworth, the bracken has gone unchecked and has invaded miles and miles of middle fell-land, often skirmishing below the fell-walls to colonize fields which were once under cultivation.

For those who think of the Lakes merely as a series of views the bracken is one of the glories of the district. It gives colour to the scene at all times of the year, except in July and August, when it is a dead-green, waist-high, sour-smelling jungle, singing with clegs and slashing at hands that grasp it. In September it gets its first buttering of yellow, and from then until May it glad-rags the fells with daubs and stripings of red and brown. There is a time late in May when the slopes still carry the brown of autumn but with a thread of green from the six-inch new fronds so that they look as if they were wrapped in shot-silk.

Yet the spread of the bracken is a sign of the near-bankruptcy of the hill-farmer. If oaks were the "climax" vegetation of the dales, then bracken is the anticlimax. Much of the Lake District, especially the more exposed flanks along the coast, is turning into an eroded landscape of bare rock, scree and bracken, splendidly photogenic, but barren of human meaning.

Afforestation

Some of the harm done by the sheep may be put right by introducing cattle crossed with a Highland breed which can find pasture on the moorland of middle height. Experiments in breeding and rearing are already being made and herds of cattle can be seen on Birker Moor and around Devoke Water. But such measures can only be of minor effect. The real counter-attack against erosion must be aimed at the primary cause of the trouble—the felling of the trees and the denudation of the uplands.

This is where the Forestry Commission comes in. Of course, its main aim is not the conservation of the soil but the economic production of timber. Yet its effect on the soil—and indeed on the whole life and scenery of the Lakes—is likely to be great and has already caused much controversy.

First of all, the Commission has agreed not to buy land in the centre of the district, leaving free the main mountain block and the dales in which lie Derwentwater, Crummock, Ullswater, Grasmere and Rydal. Its older properties are in Ennerdale, around Whinlatter Pass, on the spurs of Skiddaw above Bassenthwaite, and in upper Eskdale around Hardknott. More recently it has been carrying out plantation in lower Eskdale, in Dunnerdale, in Yewdale, and all along the moors between the eastern side of Coniston Lake and the Rusland Valley. It was, in fact, the planting in Dunnerdale and Eskdale which aroused the greatest opposition, especially from that fiery Friend of the Lake District, the late H. H. Symonds.

The chief objection was to the planting of conifers, not to hardwood or deciduous trees. The Commissioners have, therefore, agreed to plant hardwood whenever they can, but this is rarely possible on the land which they own. On the wetter moorland and fellsides the dark, unvarying Sitka spruce seems about the only tree which will grow profitably.

The earlier plantations did confirm the fears of the objectors, for the trees were planted regularly, in straight rows, so that it looked as if the mountain-slopes had been combed. The planters often left wide rides (intended, no doubt, as fire breaks) which climbed vertically, in a dead straight line, for hundreds of feet, as if a mad barber had run his clippers up the fellside. This patchy, angular, green-tartan effect is particularly obtrusive in the now-maturing plantations on both sides of Bassenthwaite Lake.

Then, again, some of the spruce plantations, such as those around Whinlatter, have a dead blackness beneath their boughs which turns the stomach like a charnel-house—a blackness quite different from the cathedral gloom of the limestone yew-woods, which are equally dark but not dead. The trees, crammed together so that not a splinter of sunlight skewers through, seem to be dying as they grow, the lower boughs already brown and withered with a poisonous compost-heap of dead needles lying about the roots. There is no undergrowth, no bramble, no cherry or other berried tree, practically no bird life, and not a sound to be heard.

But the Commissioners seem to have learnt a lot from these earlier mistakes, and much of their more recent planting has been planned with the skill of a landscape gardener. Instead of setting the trees in squares and rectangles, they now let the line of planting follow the natural line of the contour. On The Hawk, for instance, a six-hundred-foot hill in the Lickle Valley above Appletreeworth Beck, the conifers surge up and break in a curving wave against the outcrop of the rock. The darker green of the trees has taken the place of the lighter green of turf, but the pattern of the fell-side is otherwise unchanged.

Again, instead of planting acres upon acres of the same tree—like vast rolls of coconut-matting laid across the fells—they are now mixing their species. They plant spruces and firs, with here and there some oak and birch. The differing blue-greens and grey-greens and yellow-greens give a pleasant variegated look to the fellside, especially when the trees are planted in irregularly-shaped clumps with a border of oaks or birches along the edges. In mid-Duddon, along the mile or so below Troutal, the Commissioners have planted the slopes as imaginatively as Capability Brown, setting mixed conifers and hardwood apparently at random along the outcrops of crag and scree, and making the river banks into a wild garden—a rock-wood, in fact.

Above all, they are now planting larch. I do not know what the commercial value of larch-wood may be, but many new larch-woods are springing up, both on the land of the Forestry Commission and on private estates. Of course, you may call the larch a foreigner if you like. Wordsworth, in his *Description of the Scenery of the Lakes*,[1] scornfully attacked all who planted the tree, calling it "less than any other pleasing", "disagreeable" in spring and "spiritless" in autumn:

[1] First published in 1810 as an introduction to the Rev. Joseph Wilkinson's *Select Views in Cumberland, Westmorland, and Lancashire.*

A moment's thought will show that if ten thousand of this spiky tree . . . are stuck in at once upon the side of a hill, they can grow up into nothing but deformity.

But, surely, Wordsworth was wrong, and the larch, though not indigenous, has made itself thoroughly at home in the dales. Its April green is the quickest among the fells, stinging one into an awareness of spring as it gushes up the gills like a backwash of the beck. In winter its chalky-yellow or near-purple smudges a softness over the diamond-blue hardness of the rocks. And no other tree smells so strongly of Easter.

The real importance of afforestation is that it is an attempt to slow down the process of erosion and the impoverishment of the soil, and also to keep the district economically alive instead of letting it become entirely dependent on the tourist. Of course, there are objections even to this, the most serious coming from the sheep-farmers. For whatever harm the sheep may have done to the Lake landscape they are now an essential part of it, and no one wants to lose them. They must remain on all the central fells, and also in the afforested areas above the height of practical planting. The argument of the farmers is that the sheep cannot exist on the upper fell-land alone. They need the better mountain pastures for lambing-time and it is precisely these which are taken up by the new trees. Without such pastures, they argue, the rearing of Herdwicks will become unprofitable, the specialist Herdwick farms in the dales will die out, and the breed will deteriorate and disappear.

Another argument against the forests is that they put up "Private" notices and deny access to many miles of fell-country. Now, since I have been for many years a persistent and conscientious trespasser, this argument moves me less, though I have to admit that the wire-netting fences are alien and unpleasing. I am grateful, too, to the new forests for providing cover and breeding grounds for woodland birds and wild mammals, especially deer— i.e. both the fallow deer which is common around Morecambe Bay, being preserved on several of the country-house estates, and the native red deer, which still lives in a wild state at Martindale and wanders over many parts of Westmorland and High Furness.

And, even when I do not like the look of the plantations, I cannot regard them as a permanent blot on the scene. For trees are a crop—they are planted in order to be chopped down. And when those which are now being planted are eventually felled—or maybe the next crop but one is felled—then we are likely to find the fellside richer in soil and, after a season or two, more abundant in flowers.[1] To my mind what we are being asked to do is to resign our claim to the enjoyment of the open fell-land so that future generations may find it fatter and healthier and more like its old self. The trouble, of course, is that we cannot be sure there are going to be any future generations.

Reservoirs

Before passing to the more humdrum and everyday marks of man, let us look at the most spectacular scenic changes brought about in recent times. This is not the place to argue of the rightness or wrongness of large reservoirs in the Lake District, though it is surely beyond argument that we should have no more of them. No doubt we must expect some modification and extension of means of taking water from some of the lakes—Ennerdale, for instance, supplies water to Whitehaven without having suffered much harm. But we must allow no more major valleys to be dammed and flooded: there is just not enough of the Lake District left to throw any more of it away.

On the other hand, the reservoirs we already have are here to stay. No one is going to pull the plug out of Thirlmere or Haweswater. They are permanent or nearly permanent in a way that plantations are not, and we had better accept them and get along with them as well as we can.

We have to admit, first of all, that they are by no means ugly. The smaller reservoirs, indeed, are often lively and attractive, adding the sparkle of water to dull, humped moorland. Tarn Hows, for instance, one of the most notoriously pretty places in the district, is an artificial lake, though not—admittedly—a reservoir. Nor is Thirlmere ugly, if we forget what it used to be. The trouble with Thirlmere, is not that it is a reservoir, but that it is a municipal park.

On the Helvellyn side it is bordered by the busiest road in the district. On the western and less frequented side, Manchester has

[1] One danger, however, is that the first flowers to gain a hold after felling may be not native plants, but opportunist interlopers such as rosebay willowherb.

set a carriage way winding among conifers, and edged by walls
neat as a stone fire-place. The effect is paper-planned, so prim, that
you expect to find a public convenience behind each screen of
trees.[1] Manchester, admittedly, is trying to do its best by Thirlmere. The *Guardian* ran a competition for ideas on the way this
should be done. Suitable and likely suggestions included the felling of some of the trees or the replacement of the spruce by larch;
the opening of new footpaths; the pulling down of the walls
along the western road, together with its possible closure to
motor traffic. Eventually the public will be given a better chance
to see the thing of beauty that Thirlmere still is. But they will not
be able to see it as a living lake.

This same change of character from lake to reservoir is even
more obvious in the case of Haweswater, which does not look as
if it had ever been a lake. The water lies trapped unnaturally in
its drowned valley. The shores are almost dead straight and lined
with what at a distance looks like a huge concrete kerb. There is
no village, there are no farms and there is only one hotel. The only
road runs up the Swindale side, and is strictly blocked off from
the water-line, offering no temptations to picnickers. Visitors
who come by car have really to go out of the Lake District
altogether in order to get here, passing through the scruffy, powdery limestone country around Bampton. The road runs for three
or four miles between the steep, lumpy, almost-cragless sides of
a dale which is surely the most monotonous of any in the district,
and then, at the water-head, it stops dead.

And at this point you begin to wonder whether Manchester
Corporation may not have saved this valley by damming it.
For ahead of you is a magnificent dale-head, surpassed only by
that of Wasdale. The crags of Harter Fell bludgeon themselves
into the over-dale air, while the track divides into two, passing,
on the one side of the peak, to Longsleddale and, on the other
side, to Kentmere. It is a tremendous display of violent, empty
landscape, with not a single intrusive building and not a fag-end
littering the turf.

Yet you feel that something is wrong. It is not just that the
village of Mardale is below the waters, its church sunk too late
to have gathered legends of ghostly bells. It is not that the shore-

[1] It is, of course, one of the disadvantages of water-catchment areas that you
do not.

line of detritus disfigures the view, since at the top end this is not much to be noticed. It is rather that the transition from open fell to closed water is too abrupt. The marginal quarter of a mile or so is missing. We have neither the characteristic dale-head delta of burnet meadows, shillough and willows, nor the upland tarn fringe of mosses and reeds. So that what we see is not a dale with a lake in it, but a group of fells plunged up to the waist in cold water.

It is from precisely this that we must be sure to save Bannisdale.

VIII

THE MARK OF MAN—
ROADS, VILLAGES AND TOWNS

The Older Roads

BEFORE the eighteenth century, dale cottages were mostly built of turf and cobbles so that little of them remains; even many of the stone-built farms and manor-houses have fallen into ruin. But roads have a way of living on, whether they turn into a motor-highway or linger like a ghost-story as a right of way between fields and allotments.

Many of the dale roads must have kept to almost exactly the same route for centuries. Ten or twelve years ago they still ran between the same walls, skirted the same rocks, and wound through the same gates to the same farms, often actually passing through the farm-yards. Today, the main roads up and down the dales have become well-used tourist routes. The surface is good, the narrower places have been eased out, and the gates are being replaced by cattle-grids.

To get some idea of the old dale routes we must leave the metalled roads and go on to the tracks which are now the possession of the walker—Styhead Pass or Walna Scar, to take two of the better known. It is important to remember that these were roads and not just paths—the normal routes for shepherds and pedlars on foot and for gentry and visitors on horseback.

Pack-horse Bridges

After the Restoration, traders began to come to the dales in greater numbers—wool-buyers and weavers, tin and copper miners, colliers, import merchants from Whitehaven and smugglers from Ravenglass. They travelled with strings of ponies along the west coast and over the dale passes, and it was largely for them that the dale bridges were built—generally, though not quite accurately, called "pack-horse bridges". Usually they are stone bridges of one sharply-humped arch, with walls on either side and a narrow track between. Some were merely a clapper bridge of slate slabs laid from boulder to boulder across the beck. Slater's Bridge,[1] in Little Langdale, combines the two forms, being half of it humped and half of it flat flagstone.

Few of the bridges are older than the eighteenth century but they have the timeless look of the rock. When they cross a shallow beck, heaving up from flat fields, they seem rather lonely and lost. But when they are flung across a rocky cavern—as with Birks Bridge in Dunnerdale or High Sweden Bridge in Scandale—then they are as lively as the beck itself. The stones have a thick green pelt of spleenwort, wall-rue and rusty-backs, and the flood water froths up to the chin of the arches—at Birks, recently damaged by flood, the walls have little perforations, so that the water may pass over the bridge as well as under it.

There is nothing archaic about these bridges. When carriages and heavier traffic came on the roads, it was easy to develop a stronger and wider bridge of the same pattern—that by the mill over Whelan Beck at Boot in Eskdale shows the transition to the new type. In fact, the single stone arch might well be considered by modern builders whenever a small bridge is needed. There is a good twentieth-century example just below the National Trust property around the Duddon Gorge, where it has replaced an ugly wooden structure. Here the newness of the slate has already worn off, and the bridge gives a grand view of the boulders where weasels run, and of the hazels, rowans and oaks which dribble down the steep river-banks, changing greens like the water. It is a thoroughly practical piece of local workmanship, and, anyway, those who do not like it can use the stepping-stones a few yards lower down.

The Motor Roads

Twenty years ago one could say that the new roads were not very different from the old ones, but the enormous increase in motor traffic is bringing about a great change. So far the standardized ugliness of the arterial road at its worst has not yet appeared in the centre of Lakes. The main road from the south, by Kendal, Windermere and Thirlmere, has something of this character in parts, and so has the east-west road from Whitehaven through Keswick to Penrith, and both are threatened with still worse development. And the road from Levens Bridge through the

[1] Its name means that it was used by the quarrymen.

Lythe Valley, which is being used to relieve congestion in Kendal, has hacked its new way brutally through the hedges and meadows of the lower reaches of the River Gilpin. But most of the roads are still unobtrusive, at least when they are fairly empty of traffic.

The trouble, of course, is that during the holiday months they are not empty of traffic, and many of them become so packed with cars that from above they look as if they were over-run with a plague of vari-coloured beetles. Then comes the demand for the road to be widened, but road widening inevitably means more cars and possibly coaches, so that the last state, like that of the man with the seven devils, is worse than the first.

As yet, however, the dale roads have not been bulldozed into concreteformity, and can still be enjoyed by a motorist who comes out of season. Best of all, for the pleasures of driving, are the roads along the more wooded lakes—Ullswater, Derwentwater (especially on the Barrow Bay side), Coniston (on the Brantwood side), and Esthwaite (on either side). Most of these do not run along the water-edge, but dodge round knolls and copses, approaching the water and sheering off, nosing up, sniffing and bounding away like a courting collie. The road and lake are in league with one another, yet the road is not assertive, you do not see much of it at a time, and from above it is scarcely to be noticed.

It is useless to tell many people not to come to the Lakes in the holiday season since that is the only time they *can* come. Luckily, the idea that all the roads in the district are swarming with traffic is far from true. Especially away from the main tourist centres, there are miles and miles of minor roads which are rarely discovered by the visitor. I have sat beside such a road on a Whit Monday afternoon—among some of the most agreeable volcanic rock in Cumberland, with ten miles of open sea on one side of me and ten miles of open fell on the other—and counted two cars in four hours. You can find many such roads in the smaller valleys which run down to the west coast or to Morecambe Bay, and in the country north of Skiddaw and that east of Kirkstone. Even in the busiest parts there are often alternative routes. A glance at a one-inch map, for instance, will quickly show that there are four roads from Cockermouth to Bassenthwaite, one of which is usually about as packed as Blackpool promenade.

Yet the other three, even at the height of the season, carry little traffic and are only a mile or two longer.

But it is from the 2½-inch maps that the motorist can really learn how to dodge the traffic. Here he will find scores of small roads running up the side-valleys to remote farms and houses. Many have only been tarmacked within the last year or so, and some have only two parallel strips of metalling with the grass growing between. With the help of these even someone who can walk only a short distance can reach some of the loneliest and wildest country in the district. Then there are the roads laid down for the Forestry Commission, some of which are open to the public, and there are also private roads to reservoirs, quarries, mines and the like, for the use of which permission will often be given. Of course you do not use such roads if your car is as wide as a bus, or if you are not prepared to stop and back when you meet a farm tractor or works lorry. The roads, after all, were made for the local people, not for the stranger.

Coast Roads

Along the Cumberland coast south of Whitehaven there is scarcely a sea-side stretch of road more than a mile long. In Furness, from Rampside to Bardsea, there is a fine road beside the limestone shore looking across Morecambe Bay. But in the rest of the bay—north of, say, Silverdale—the roads make great scallops round the heads of the estuaries, and in Cumberland they keep two to four miles from the sea, bumping over the lower spurs of the hills or along tracks which once joined farm to farm. The motorist in a hurry on the bucking-bronco of a road from Gosforth to Silecroft and Millom must be exasperated to see— often only a hundred yards away—the dead level coastal plain along which the railway now runs. The reason why the road avoids this seemingly obvious route lies back in the Ice Age, for the retreating ice deposited a long, broken ridge of boulder clay and gravel along the line of the shore, behind which there developed a parallel trough of swamp and mud. And, since in pre-Macadam days mud was the traveller's worst hindrance, the road took to the hills. Eighteenth-century tourists praised the Lake District roads precisely because they were steep and stony and free from mud.

The absence of a coast road has had conflicting results. It has certainly helped to keep the South Cumberland coastline comparatively unspoiled, but, at the same time, it has held back industrial development in West Cumberland. So that during the last three or four decades many schemes have been put forward for a new road from Lancaster to Whitehaven. The least ambitious of these proposes to follow the general line of the old road, bypassing the villages, swinging clear of the flanks of the hills, and building new bridges over the rivers rather nearer the sea than are the present ones. The larger schemes include bridging the Esk–Irt estuary, bridging or damming the Duddon between Askam and Millom, and reclaiming vast areas of Morecambe Bay by means of embankments across the estuaries of the Leven and the Kent. One scheme envisages an enormous embankment from Aldingham to Hest Bank, isolating the Cartmel peninsula from the sea, and leaving Grange-over-Sands stranded on the edge of miles of flat fen-land.

The scheme is not new, being first brought forward in the eighteenth century, while in 1837 George Stephenson made an "Oracular Survey" for two railway routes from Lancaster to Carlisle, one over the fells and one along the coast. The next year came John Hague's "Most Magnificent Project" of reclaiming Morecambe Bay and the Duddon Estuary—a project taken up with some enthusiasm, but dropped because it was too vague and costly. Later, John Abel Smith planned to run a railway ferry from Fleetwood to Barrow, and got as far as building a pier at Roa Island before the plan was dropped. Then, in the 1860s, a start was made to bridge the Duddon. Powers were obtained from Parliament, tenders were invited, and building material was assembled at Askam. This scheme was dropped like the others, and, though no reason was given, it was thought that the promoters feared the development of the port of Whitehaven at the expense of that of Barrow.[1] But though the bridge was never built the plan brought a certain advantage to the people of the Duddon Estuary, since the fare for the journey was based not on the distance of the actual track by Kirkby and Foxfield, but on the distance by the bridge which was never built. Until fairly recently the journey from Askam to Millom remained the cheapest of its length in England.

[1] See: *Early Railway History in Furness*, J. Melville and J. L. Hobbs (1951); and *Furness and the Industrial Revolution*, J. D. Marshall (Barrow, 1958).

A farm near Loweswater

Railways

Apart from the main lines by the coast and the narrow-gauge line in Eskdale, there are only four railways in the Lakes—the Workington–Penrith line, which passes along the shore of Bassenthwaite; the Foxfield–Coniston line; the Ulverston–Lake Side line, linking with the steamers on Windermere; and the Kendal–Windermere line. The first three of these are now closed, except for the Keswick to Penrith section of the northern line. The harm done by such closures is immense. It isolates villages, throws still more traffic on to the roads, obliges the bus companies to run services along unsuitable routes, and forces the highway authorities to make improvements on roads which had better have been left as they were. In the case of the Coniston line, the closure almost coincided with the opening of a central secondary modern school for the area, so that children from Broughton and Torver have to be taken every morning by bus along a road which is sometimes steep, always narrow, and often icy in winter. There has already been one accident to the school bus and parents appealed in vain for the return of the train or for the use of a rail-car on the old railway track. The best suggestion, which now seems likely to be carried out, would seem to be to turn the old track into a road, perhaps a one-way route, which should give an easy, gently-curving way of access to Coniston and take many of the dangers from the present road.

It is odd, now, to think how indignant Ruskin was when the Coniston railway was first proposed, for this line is so unobtrusive, so skilfully screened by trees, that you hardly notice it. By means of it you could creep right into the heart of the Lakes without the least fuss or hurry or effort. For forty years it was my regular way of approach to the central fells—setting off at the windy, sand-side station of Foxfield, and moving as if in a shallow trench between rocks and woods until Coniston Lake appeared on the one side of the train and the Old Man on the other. When I travelled on this line on the day of its final run, in October 1958, I felt that the true road to the Lakes had been fenced off, even though you can make the journey by the other road in just about the same time.

Like the Coniston line, that from Greenodd to Lake Side (on Windermere) is skilfully hidden from view, and so, too, is the line from Keswick to Threlkeld. There are places where, from

Yew Tree Farm near Coniston

above, the engine smoke seems to issue mysteriously from fissures in the earth. Even where the line is bare and unconcealed, it is not what William Gilpin, the High Priest of the Picturesque, would have called "disgusting", while the trains themselves look far more at home on the fells than many human beings—whether trumpeting down the express lines from Shap like prehistoric pachyderms or panting up the hill from Penruddock to Troutbeck.

In the lowlands, as in the rest of England, the railway is a familiar and traditional part of the scene. I will not pretend that it improved the shore of Bassenthwaite, or that it does not draw too rigid and heavy a line along stretches of the coast between Seascale and St. Bees. But on the whole it is friendly, adaptable and good-mannered, though, of course, already old-fashioned. The embankments are covered with flowers—primrose, dogdaisy and wild strawberry—and in early summer the despised ribwort plantain gives a sugar-dusting of white to the green. In waste places, among sidings and loading-sheds, there is rosebay and butterbur, white wild carrot and yellow wild parsnip; and in ditches at the side of the track, yellow iris, purple loosestrife, and the greater willowherb or codlins-and-cream. Even the cinders have their own weeds, such as the small purple toadflax, the seeds of which may perhaps be wafted along in the draught from passing trains. Such pleasures are perhaps for the very patient or the very short-sighted, but even the most impetuous and eagle-eyed must agree that the views down the lower reaches of many of the western rivers (the Mite, the Esk, the Leven, the Bela, the Kent) would lose their final dramatic climax if the railway viaducts were taken down.

Cottages and Farms

Perhaps the sub-heading should really be "Walls". For the stone wall is the basic unit of Lake architecture. Cottages, farms, manor-houses and even villages are stone walls set together at angles and roofed over in parts. The walls, as I said in Chapter II, were mostly built in the eighteenth or nineteenth centuries when labour was cheap, and they are falling to bits in this twentieth century when labour is dear. The farmer and the forester find it both cheaper and quicker to set up a new stake-and-wire fence than to repair an old wall. And as the 60- and 80-acre holdings are merged into larger farms, the great boundary walls of the open fellsides are no longer of any use, and will soon collapse into long rigs of heaped scree, and the art of walling with the unshaped stone will be forgotten. The art of walling with the shaped stone, however, is still widely practised. Many of the new walls along the improved National Park roads are of this kind, and though the stone looks raw at present it will soon weather comfortably into the landscape.

There is also another type of slate walling, less often seen and confined usually to the valleys, which consists of a fence made of large slabs of slate set up on end like thin tombstones, the edge of one just touching that of the next. These slates are not bound or fastened together in any way,[1] though sometimes a thorn hedge is built close enough to give extra support to the stones. Such fences are particularly common in the Coniston and Hawkshead districts and speak of a time when the local people cared more for their own in-take or kitchen garden than for the wild, unrentable fell-tops.

So, too, it is with the cottages. They were not built for the sake of the view; nor were they built to be looked at. They were essentially homes, built to give shelter in what then was—and on a November night still is—a bleak and inhospitable climate. They are therefore as inconspicuous as possible. The farms of the upper fells squat and cower in the dips of little gills or corries— (the home of Wordsworth's "Solitary" near Blea Tarn is a well-known example)—or huddle like a sheep close to an over-hanging rock. They are hewn out of the rock and the people who live in them are still, in a way, cave-dwellers. The walls are thick, doorways and windows low and deep-set. On the edge of the sandstone districts the roofs were once covered with huge sandstone flags, sometimes four feet square, but these have mostly been re-slated with the green stone of Honister or dark grey Kirkby Roundheads, though Welsh slates are to be found in the nineteenth-century industrial towns round the rim of the area.

In the dales, the cottages often stand toeing the road, with not even room for a hydrangea between wall and tarmac. Sometimes, where the road has been widened, a cottage will jut out like

---

[1] In this they differ from the rather similar slate fences found in Welsh quarry villages where the slabs are much narrower and are bound together at the top by a wire or cable.

a bus which has got jammed, while at the old vicarage of Sea-thwaite[1] in Dunnerdale, part of the outer wall of the ground floor seems to have been carved off to allow traffic to worm round the corner. Dry-stone walls do not always stand up very well to the tremors of traffic, for which reason—as well as for extra protection from the weather—many are now plastered or rough cast and whitewashed or colour-washed. Some of the ice-cream pinks and blues which are appearing in the district are about as pleasant to look at as a half-sucked lollipop thrown away in a hedge. But in the Coniston district there used to be a shade of dark orange, less popular nowadays, which settles into the landscape like the colour of autumn oak.

The farms are of any shape. The house may be stiff and angular, with three windows up, two and a door down, and chimneys sticking up at either end like a dog pricking its ears. In the seventeenth century they were usually only one room thick, and there are still some farms remaining (such as Bield in Little Langdale)[2] where at least one of the rooms runs the full depth of the house from back to front. Some of the eighteenth-century buildings hide a certain Georgian elegance on the inside, and some have their entire front elevation tile-hung with local slates, like a perpendicular slate roof—e.g. Hesketh Hall at Broughton Mills near Broughton-in-Furness.

Some, such as the magnificent Coniston Old Hall on the banks of Coniston Lake, retain the massive round chimney-stacks of the late medieval fortified manors—almost as massive as the pillars of Durham Cathedral, though built to hold nothing up. Nearly all have a porch over the front door—usually no more than two foot of wall jutting out on either side, with a little peaked roof on top, or perhaps one flagstone laid level across.

The older village inns are scarcely distinguishable from cottages or farms, and until recently, many of them *were* farms. In the eighteenth and early nineteenth centuries, when most people passed through the district on foot, there were many small and miserable farm-inns where travellers could get a pint of sour beer, a slice of bacon or a pot of porridge, and maybe a bed for the night. Most of them closed down years ago—as did Wordsworth's

[1] The living has been combined with that of Ulpha.
[2] The home of Delmar Banner, painter, and his wife, Josephine de Vasconcellos, sculptor.

Dove Cottage which takes its name from the inn it formerly was. But those which still remain now find themselves caught up into the new tourist prosperity. Even in some of the more remote dales you can find village inns which boast of their wine list and offer a menu in French. No one is going to complain about the improvement in the food, but catering of this kind is a cosmopolitan profession, so that many of the smarter inns and hotels are being taken over by off-comers with little knowledge of the district and none of the local people. There is a famous story of a party of students who came to "The Traveller's Rest" at Ulpha and found an apparently uneducated landlord speaking an uncouth Cumbrian dialect. To pull his leg they sent him a letter in Latin asking for their bill, and were surprised to get it in Greek with a note pointing out the mistakes in their own Latin. Today the surprise would be to find a landlord who could speak the dialect.

Yet there still remain inns like "The Woolpack" at Eskdale which, in spite of all the comforts they can offer to the visitor, have not broken with the local community from which they sprang. In some of them the Shepherds' Meet is held once a year, and the dialect clicks across the tables in the bar-parlour and wrestling trophies hang beside the dart-board. Others—"The Wasdale Head" and the old "Dungeon Ghyll" in particular—have become unofficial headquarters of the rock-climbers, where you risk breaking your neck from falling over the ropes and boots which lie about the hall. And in many of them, at almost any time of the day, you can get the ham and eggs which, more than any other food, go best with the Cumbrian scene.

Villages

To a visitor from the South of England the dale villages often do not look like villages at all. They are more like a pre-industrial ribbon development—small terraces and single cottages strung out along the side of the road. There is no village green with church and pub and manor house standing round. The church is sometimes half a mile or more away and the vicarage even further. The reason is partly that the narrowness of the dale gives no room for the village to spread width-ways, and partly that the district is comparatively free from the feudalism which has dominated village-life in many other parts of the country. Not only in the dales, but along the coast, and in many parts of the surrounding lowlands there is little sign of the power of the heriditary landowner. Appleby has developed under the benevolent shadow of Lady Anne Clifford's castle; Cark and Cartmel owe much to Holker Hall; and Askham is almost an extra-mural extension of Lowther Castle, even though the castle itself is now only a remnant of mock-gothic stage-scenery. But these are exceptions.

There are, of course, castles and pele towers in the Lakes which have become the dwellings of the wealthy, and there are old fortified farm-houses which have gone on being farm-houses and refused to become mansions. But the Great House of Trollope's England and the half-a-crown-a-time Stately Home of ours is almost entirely missing from the dales. Instead we get those nineteenth-century country houses which were built for rich cotton merchants and the like to retire in. The style came from that of the more grandiose Victorian villa, and retains a likeness to it in the many gables, the steep-pitched roofs and the bay or turret windows. Brantwood—which Ruskin bought without bothering to come up to see it—moves towards the historical pageant with hints of a Highland fortress, while at Randy Pike near Hawkshead, once owned by a friend of mine, the style is so obstinately whimsical that a guest used to have to walk along a corridor, down the stairs, across the floor of the house, upstairs again and along another corridor to get to the bathroom.

Yet for all their period eccentricities such houses have grown into the scene because they have been given a skin-graft of native stone. Rock-like and lichened in walls and roof, and with their woodwork painted dark green—though, today, a dark red and a criminal metallic blue are often to be seen—they almost disappear behind the yews and firs and enormous hay-stacks of rhododendrons.

Now when a northcountryman walks into a village in the Home Counties, he feels, often, that it is too good to be true. The grass is too neat; the paint too spick; the walls too span. It is a towns-man's village, preserved like a toy and housing scarcely one born-and-bred countryman among its entire population. The Lake villages do not look like that. They escaped the first explosion of extra-suburban building in the twenties and thirties, since that was a time when there was not much money in the north, while post-war developments have been carefully watched by the rural councils. Nowhere in the Lakes do you feel that a village lives under the magnetic pull of the town, except perhaps around Kendal which, after all, is a home product.

Yet, quite apart from the main tourist centres—which are growing more and more into mere service stations for urban England—there is no village in the district which does not feel to some extent the impact and pressure of town and industry. I think of those I know best—mostly on my own side of the area.

First of all there are those villages which have been carved lengthwise in half by a trunk-line of traffic. The result is often tragic. Greenodd, set where the River Crake from Coniston flows into the tidal waters of the River Leven, must once have been a quiet, melancholy village, with the estuarine damps misting up the bracken slopes and the beeches above Penny Bridge. Today, on a busy afternoon, you may have to wait a quarter of an hour to cross the road, while the motor-cyclists batter themselves to death a couple of hundred yards away at Legbarrow Point. The Lakes are not on the direct route from any of the greater populated areas to the holiday towns, so they have been saved from the fate of Kirkby Stephen, mid-way between County Durham and Blackpool, where the main street has become little more than a stopping-spot for coaches. Yet the Lakes, too, have their pull, and the churning and shunting of cars and lorries along the approach routes can deafen and coarsen a village without putting much in its pocket. Milnthorpe, once the port of Westmorland, has now a backward-and-forward two-handled saw of traffic slicing it open. Heversham, a mile further north, is mercifully saved by a by-pass, though it is still so close to the road as to have the air of an elegant lay-by. Levens and Brigsteer, a little further up the estuary in a tributary valley, are right off the main road, untroubled by through traffic and mostly undiscovered by visitors. Kirkby-in-Furness has a road driving right through the middle of its triangle of hamlets—Beckside, Soutergate and Sandside—without, in fact, its hitting any one of them. Gosforth, at the crossing of the Whitehaven–Millom and the Seascale–Wasdale roads has had the good fortune to be built along the least busy of the four arms.

Of course, in the centre of the tourist area, no village is left alone. Watendlath, once almost proverbial for its inaccessibility, is now associated with one of Hugh Walpole's more preposterous heroines, so that the narrow road from Derwentwater is sometimes clogged with cars. But there are many others, in the less advertised areas, which are quite left off the visiting lists: Great Urswick and Scales in Low Furness; Hesket Newmarket and Uldale, back of Skiddaw; Sandwith, Haile and Beckermet near the coast. None of these—except perhaps those behind Skiddaw—have the far-away, three-generations-behind look of the picture-calendar village. Beckermet (like Gosforth) is the home of many of the scientists at Calder Hall; Haile lies almost underneath the spoil-heap of an old mine; Sandwith, once a collier's and quarryman's terrace with its mahogany sandstone streaked and grimed with hardship, now has the busy Marchon Chemical workings almost in its back gardens. All three villages house men and women who work at Whitehaven, just as Urswick and Scales house workers from Barrow. Yet none of them look as if they had been bought up by towns and turned into outer-suburbs, for it is not, on the whole, the townsmen who have gone to live in the villages but the villagers who have found work in the towns.

Industry in the Lakes

Nor is there anything new in this. For if you look in the villages of the district you will find that often they have grown up, not around farming or marketing, but around some local industry. Mining became the most important of these as early as the reign of the first Elizabeth, with centres at Keswick and Coniston, and though it shifted to the coast in the nineteenth century its place was taken by quarrying. Flakes of Langdale, Tilberthwaite and Kirkby Moor were hammered on to the roofs of hundreds of thousands of houses in the industrial north, and the demand gave a new prosperity to villages like Chapel Stile and Coniston. Many of these quarries are now closed down, though without anywhere creating those battlefield landscapes of rubble and ruin which are found in the old quarrying districts of Wales. Cumberland slate is still in reasonable demand, however, not only as local building material, but also as a handsome stone-facing which can be used most effectively in modern architecture. Stone from Broughton Moor, in North Lancashire, has been exported to Australia and some of it is used in the new Coventry Cathedral.

Nor is slate the only stone quarried in the Lakes. Shap, Threl-keld and Eskdale continue to give granite for the roads, while the limestone quarries on the rim of the area provide vast amounts of material for the blast-furnaces. At Carnforth you can see an entire hillside being gradually gnawed away to help to make steel.

And in one area the iron industry has made a more endearing mark on the Lake scene. For in Low Furness, where, on the whole, the mines were developed ahead of those of Cumberland, the early blast-furnaces or forges depended on charcoal. So that in nearly all the little valleys running down to Morecambe Bay there grew up a colony of wood-cutters and charcoal burners (Ashburner is a very common name in the area), together with small saw-mills, usually driven by water-power. And beside the saw-mills there sprang up bobbin-mills, worked by water to supply the cotton trade of Lancashire. As a child I found something strange in the idea of bobbin-mills, as if they might be run by gnomes or dwarfs, so that when I heard that there were bobbin-mills at Ulpha in Dunnerdale I was quite ready to believe my father when he assured me that there were treacle-mines there too.

The bobbin-mills and most of the saw-mills are now derelict, but one other industry derived from charcoal-burning has not yet died out. This is the making of swills. The swill is a large basket, shaped like a coracle, and made entirely by hand. The rim is formed of a branch of a tree, about a thumb's thickness and usually with the bark left on, while the body is made of strips of wood, two inches wide at the centre, bent and plaited together. The whole is not nearly so heavy as might be expected and it is quite exceptionally strong. The swill was first used by the ash-burners, but is now popular with farmers, especially for gathering potatoes. Farmers' wives use it on washing-day, and there can be no more serviceable clothes-basket than a swill, for whichever way you put it down it swings on its round bottom and rights itself like a loaded chess-man. It stands up to the wet and has such obvious practical value that there are no signs as yet of its giving way to mass-produced baskets imported from outside. Some of the swill-makers occasionally turn their hands to other products. If the page I am now writing does not please me it will be thrown into a swill waste-paper-basket, made some years ago by one of the younger craftsmen, an excellent bass singer, then working at

Broughton-in-Furness. Luckily, though swills are very useful for gardeners and housewives they are hardly the kind of knick-knackery that pleases the eyes of the visitors so that swill-making has not yet been captured by the sham bucolics of the tourist trade.

Mining Towns

Many of the present-day manufactures in the Lake villages have little obvious connection with the district—paper-making at Burneside, carpets at Burton-in-Kendal, washing-blue at Backbarrow. But mining is rooted in the rock, and though it has almost disappeared from the central dales, it has stamped its character on two of the most important tourist centres, Coniston and Keswick.[1]

Copper has been mined at Coniston on and off for about two thousand years, and as recently as the last century the mines employed nine hundred men and boys. At the time of the German miners, the copper ore was carted over Dunmail Raise to be smelted at Keswick, but later it was carried down the lake by boat to Nibthwaite, carted to Greenodd or Ulverston, and thence went by sea to Wales.

The mines are now closed and the mine buildings became, for a time, a Youth Hostel, though the rock still gives employment to local men at the famous Broughton Moor quarries. The main livelihood of the villages probably comes from the visitors, but Coniston has been able to absorb these without rolling down its shirtsleeves. There are a few new houses, rather neatly tucked away, and a small council housing estate, not tucked away at all, but, at the same time, no great eye-sore. There is a new modern comprehensive school, serving the youth of High Furness, a coffee bar, serving the same, and the Ruskin Museum with its set of musical rocks. Outside, the banners of the ice-cream companies make the streets look as if they were the start of an old-fashioned Sunday school procession. Yet Coniston remains an honest slate village, plain but not fussy, turning its back on the lake, and

[1] One might also add the name of Alston, though this is not really in the Lake area. Here, nearly a thousand feet up in the East Cumbrian Pennines, lead mining continued until the twenties and thirties, after which it ebbed away leaving a stranded town whose grim oddity scarcely betrays the poverty and distress it held only a generation ago.

looking to the Old Man for work and shelter. At one time the fell gave light, also, since Church Beck was harnessed to a dynamo, and the village enjoyed electricity long before the industrial towns on the coast.

Keswick has much the same history as Coniston, except that the mines lie further away from the town, scattered among the fells round about. At one time it was the centre of a small wool trade, and then came the prosperous period of mining for copper, lead and silver, followed, later, by the manufacture of black-lead pencils made from the Borrowdale plumbago. Before it was worked out, the plumbago or graphite mine, near Seathwaite, was one of the wonders of the Lakes visited by nearly all the tourists, including Thomas Gray. The "wad" or black-lead was found in sops or pipes of various sizes and dimensions. In the eighteenth century it was used for casting round-shot and cannon balls, and was so valuable that guards were set round the mine and the miners were stripped and searched when they left work. One deposit, found in 1803, yielded thirty and a quarter tons, worth (at that time) about £100,000.[1]

The older part of Keswick takes its shape and personality from this earlier industrial era. Round the market place are the courts and alleys where the workers lived, packed tight as the pencils, and there is also the business-like Moot Hall, a building so slim that you expect a run-away bus to split on it like a ship on a rock.

But this older working-town Keswick is disappearing beneath the over-night luggage of the new tourism. Shopkeepers, café proprietors and hoteliers own the main streets now. Admittedly they have not done their worst, though some excessively ugly shop-fronts have been introduced, and there have been attempts, here and there, to jazz-up the town as if it were the promenade at Morecambe. I once complained that there was a blur of damp good taste over Keswick, but this is being blown away in the exuberance of the new campers, from the North East and else-where, who know their Pop better than their Wordsworth. Yet, in the dining-room of "The Royal Oak" you can find a set of stained glass windows, each with an appropriate quotation, dedicated to the Lake Poets, including—oddly enough—P. B. Shelley. Perhaps, if they had waited a year or two they could

[1] John Postlethwaite: *Mines and Mining in the Lake District* (Whitehaven). This fascinating book is one of the classics of Lake literature.

have filled in the final window without having to go out of the district. [1]

It is easy to make fun of Keswick and a Cumbrian with any self-respect feels almost obliged to do so. But it is quite unfair. For what has happened to the town is not its own fault but the result of modern man's inability to enjoy himself without making a mess of the spot where he does so. The fate of Keswick was decided when the first eighteenth-century travellers crossed over Dunmail Raise in search of the Picturesque. [2] Its situation is magnificent. No other town in the district—none, in fact, in England—is so fitted to become a tourist metropolis. The dale, the two lakes, the fells are laid out before you, giving up their great views without asking the payment of five minutes' effort. Skiddaw, the most obligingly demonstrative mountain in Cumberland, is so accessible that the Victorian ladies ascended it on pony-back. The town itself is not without beauty. Visitors of all kinds are accommodated and made to feel at home, from young men carrying guitars, to evangelical clergymen attending the annual convention in what—perhaps wrongly—has been called "the largest marquee in the world". To live and die in Keswick would be a happy lot for any man, though happiest for those who lived there not less than fifty years ago.

The Wool Towns

The manufacture of woollen goods began in Kendal some six hundred years ago. John Kempe, of Flanders, came over to England in 1331 to introduce improved methods in weaving, though, in spite of Cornelius Nicholson, [3] there is no real proof that he settled in Kendal. Other Flemish weavers may have come to the town, however, for Kendal cloth was mentioned in enactments before the end of the fourteenth century, and in Tudor times the town was supplying London with much of its everyday wear—plain, hard-wearing stuff, rather coarse, and known as "Kendal cottons".

[1] The Lake Poets, however, seem to be losing value as a tourist draw. In a series of lectures, organized by the Extra-mural Department of King's College, Newcastle, and given at Keswick in the summer of 1962, it was found that those on the literary associations of the Lakes attracted much smaller audiences than those on geology, history, etc.

[2] See: N. Nicholson: *The Lakers* (Robert Hale).

[3] See: *Annals of Kendal* by Cornelius Nicholson (1861).

Most of the wool was spun by the housewives in their own homes and woven by their husbands on cottage looms, after which it went to the town, to the fulling mill and the dyer. It was for its dyes, in particular, that Kendal was famous. Its "spotted cottons"—white spotted with red, green or blue—were worn by the English bowmen at Flodden Field. Better-known still was the "Kendal Green" of Falstaff's "three misbegotten knaves" [1]—a colour obtained by dyeing the cloth first of all with the yellow of dyer's greenweed (Genista Tinctoria) and then with a blue extracted from woad. The greenweed, rather like a dwarf broom, still grows abundantly in the district.

The trade began to expand in the reign of Edward IV, encouraged by the powerful Parr family of Kendal Castle, who gave to Henry VIII the wife who was to become his widow. By her time the trade had spread into the neighbouring towns and villages—up the Kent to Staveley, down the valley to Milnthorpe, over the low hills to Windermere, and along the Rothay and the Brathay into Grasmere and Langdale. It has been estimated [2] that, in the fifteenth and early sixteenth centuries, there were at least eight walk-mills or fulling-mills in the parish of Grasmere alone.

Soon, however, the trade began to decline, and when the plague reached the district towards the end of the seventeenth century, it carried off many of the workers, especially the cottage weavers. Kendal cloth was now right out of fashion, in spite of Shakespeare's boost, though the merchants of the town were able to keep in business by diverting their goods to America to cover the modesty of the negro slaves. In the smaller towns and villages, however, the trade dwindled and dwindled until at last it disappeared almost entirely.

These smaller towns fall into two groups—those built on the slate and those built on the limestone. And the slate villages include most of the best-known tourist centres on the southern side of the Lakes: Ambleside, Grasmere, Hawkshead and Skelwith Bridge. Now when the wool industry collapsed these spots were left almost derelict. The valleys—Langdale, especially—

---

[1] *Henry IV*, Part I, Act II, Sc. iv.
[2] By Miss M. L. Armitt. See: *Fullers and Freeholders of the Parish of Grasmere*: Transactions of the Cumberland and Westmorland Archaeological Society, Vol. VIII, New Series (1908).

became what three hundred years later would have been called a Distressed Area. The population was far greater than the land could support, and there are signs of desperate attempts to plough barren patches of fellside for the sake of a handful of oats. Hawkshead still carried on its wool-market, but for the most part the towns tried to adapt themselves to the new conditions. Fulling mills were turned into tanneries, while bobbin-mills and saw-mills were set up in the old warehouses.

It was in this grim industrial perspective of prosperity, unemployment and reconstruction that the National Park villages took shape. The old mills have closed down, and the buildings have disappeared or have been altered until they are no longer recognisable, but there is still the print of the practical about the houses and streets. Ambleside has its absurd, one-up, one-down house on a bridge over the beck, built according to local legend, by a Scotsman who wanted to avoid paying land-tax[1]—a structure with a blatant quizzicality that ogles the camera. Elsewhere, the town is free from all taint of prettiness. Its buildings are solid, angular and surprisingly tall, with huge, blank gable-ends like the face of a quarry. There are alleys and arches and narrow side-streets, all so dourly mercantile that a window-box looks as impertinent as a carnation in the button-hole of an undertaker. It lies on the busiest main road in the district and receives vast numbers of visitors by land and water, yet it seems to have hung on to its independence far more stubbornly than Keswick, Bowness or Windermere Town. You feel that this is not just a place where people spend their holidays but a place where people live. One who does in fact live there told me that in summer the inhabitants lose sight of one another among the crowds of strangers, but that in October they re-emerge in the streets and meet one another again.

Ambleside is fortunate in that, though it is right in the Wordsworth country, it has few exploitable associations with the poet. For Wordsworth, like Shakespeare and Burns, gives rise to many pilgrimages on the part of non-readers. Dove Cottage gets thousands of visitors a year, many Americans[2] among them, and

[1] In fact, it was probably built as an Amusing Object to embellish an estate. The house is now owned by the National Trust.

[2] One visiting American made a present of a new car to the vicar of a local parish, "as a tribute to Wordsworth".

some venture into the Wordsworth Museum, just across the road, where there is a valuable and extremely interesting collection of manuscripts and early editions. But the popular fame of Wordsworth, even merely as the Poet Laureate of daffodils, is growing fainter. It is said that one visitor who had been shown over Dove Cottage turned to the curator asking: "Who did you say lived here?"

The other main Wordsworthian centre is Hawkshead, where the poet attended the Grammar School and lodged during term time at Anne Tyson's cottage. This is the country of the first two books of *The Prelude*—the woods around Esthwaite Water, with Windermere on one side and Yewdale and Coniston on the other, and with the Old Man, Wetherlam and the Langdale Pikes staring down into the dale. I doubt if many people go to Hawkshead now with Wordsworth in mind, especially since it has been shown that Wordsworth's lodging was not in the village at all, but about a quarter of a mile away at Colthouse.[1] Yet Hawkshead still gets its visitors, hundreds and hundreds of them, for reasons which we must now face.

Hawkshead, then, is quaint, fascinating, picturesque, old-world. It deserves all those adjectives which I have tried to keep out of this book, and, moreover, it deserves them in a deliberate and precise sense. If the word "quaint" could have all its pseudo-quaintness washed off it to mean just "quaint" again, then that is what Hawkshead would be. But unfortunately it has had to suffer the same treatment as all the other quaint villages, to be photographed and water-coloured until its individual and delicious oddity has become that of a doll's village, an exhibit in the York Museum lacking only the fluorescent lighting and the glass barriers.

Yet it is hard to see what else could have happened, for its oddness is not the kind which could easily have been adapted to present-day life. It is so small, to begin with. It had to be preserved or else to be damaged beyond all knowing. Its origin, like that of Ambleside, was in the wool trade, but its beauty as it exists today seems quite unrelated to any practical way of living. It

[1] See: *William Wordsworth: A Biography, The Early Years*, by Mary Moorman (Oxford, 1957).

It was Beatrix Potter who discovered the first evidence which led to the identification of the Colthouse cottage.

is the beauty not of purpose nor of design nor of art, but merely of accident—of narrow lanes and whitewashed walls, of cottages with stone staircases on the outside, of Flag Street and Pillar House and the "Red Lion" yard. You walk among the houses almost forgetting that they *are* houses, and seeing instead parallelograms of plaster, elephant legs of pillars, slated tunnels and angles and corners, with mauve and green shadows pinned against the whitewash. In this rather abstract way, Hawkshead manages to exist and to hang on to its beauty, but it has had to pay a great price. I am attracted to the town and always enjoy going there, but I never do so without feeling a twinge of conscience.

South and east of Kendal lies the limestone country where the villages, though they all shared in the same wool industry, have lost most of their urban manner. There are factories hidden away here and there—carpets, paper, milk products—but on the whole these villages look as townspeople think they ought to look. Milnthorpe, Heversham and Beetham all find themselves threaded on the wire-rope-way of the A6 and have not yet managed to get used to it. The people live in one century in-doors and another out. Burton is on the alternative route from Carnforth to Kendal, and, in spite of the traffic, manages to keep a stubbornly archaic frontage for the whole length of its street, with its musical-comedy square, a pillared house almost as batty as that at Hawkshead, and a cobbler's shop so small that it would all go—upstairs, downstairs, back and front—into one fair-sized room. Holme, agreeably secluded from both the main roads, is, oddly enough, the least old-fashioned-looking of the lot. Quite half the buildings are new and there is a small housing estate for the workers at the carpet factory. Yet this uncelebrated, unphotographed village is as good as any from which to bite into the real flavour of lower Kendal. There is limestone everywhere—in the church, in the field-walls, in the broken-off clints decorating cottage doors. There is grass greener than the dale grass and lambs whiter than the dale lambs, and there are cowslips—almost unknown in the slate country—along the railway embankments. There is also the old Lancaster–Kendal canal to fish in and there are its comic, leap-frog-back bridges to lean over and spit from.

But the chief of these southern wool towns lies not in the valley of the Kent but beyond Hutton Roof in the valley of the Lune. Kirkby Lonsdale does not quite belong to the Lakes. Though it

stands on the western side of the long, lush trough of the Lune, it is really part of the Pennines, the "backbone", with the mud-pies of the Howgill Fells to the north and the table-top of Ingleborough to the south. Here the landscape is broader and wider, and the streets lie open to tidal winds flowing down from the fells. It is a land less humanized than the dales of the Lake District, in spite of which Kirkby Lonsdale is as unmistakably urban as Ambleside or the smaller Hawkshead. (So, too, is the nearby Dent, just over the Yorkshire border, once the centre of a hand-knitting trade, and so small that it would fit easily into a London square.[1]) But that is about the end of any resemblance to the Lake towns, for Kirkby has more of the look of Tudor England. It is built not of slate but of limestone, and of limestone yellower than that of the Kent valley, more like the chamois-leather of the Cotswolds. It is a grave town, minding its own business and minding that business well, so that you are not surprised to learn that the area round about has produced many famous Quakers. Along the main street there is scarcely a house, an inn or a shop which does not give pleasure in its shape and companionableness. Many of the houses are of the eighteenth century or a little later, with the outlying streets sturdy and strong and often covered with a lovely rind, rich as orange peel. The Market Square is cluttered by an excessively ugly market cross, built in the form of a crown and acting now as a bus shelter. But the old cross, or part of it, can still be seen in the Swine Market, opposite Abbot's Hall—a drowsy pillar, set on steps, with a stone globe in place of its original cross-head.

Ruskin praised the view of the river from a spot just beyond the church, while the church itself is one of the most beautiful in the Carlisle diocese, with a solemn Norman west end and good Jacobean wood-carving—though, having no real chancel, it is liturgically not quite satisfactory.

The Market Towns

Such are the towns which were once apprenticed to Kendal.

---

[1] Dent has strong connections with the Lakes since it was the birthplace of Professor Adam Sedgwick, a pioneer geologist, who was the first to make a systematic study of the Lake rocks. He was a friend of Wordsworth and contributed five letters on geology to the later editions of Wordsworth's *Guide to the Lakes.*

Townend House, Troutbeck
Hawkshead Old Grammar School and Church

Today, only the master-town retains its old trade, to which it has added others, in particular the making of boots and shoes. Kendal —it was originally "Kirkby Kendal", so called to distinguish it from Kirkby Lonsdale and Kirkby Stephen—is therefore more of a manufacturing town than a country market town.

It serves the area with shops and lawyers, holds annually what it claims to be the oldest musical festival in England, and houses an adventurous art centre at Abbot Hall. Yet it is quite free of the over-bred refinement of the cathedral city or the self-conscious tweediness of the county town—and, in fact, though Kendal is the administrative centre of Westmorland, it is Appleby which is the capital. Its long main street—now, part of it, strung on to the A6 —takes a rough individuality from its hilliness and from the fact that many of the buildings still show the slate they were first made of, but its artificial smile of shop-fronts and offices is not very different from that of almost any mid-sized north-country town, the Town Hall being a typical example of Municipal Comic.

It is when you move off into the side-alleys or wynds that you find what is still left of the real Kendal. Here you walk in deep gills between the high walls of warehouses or the sides of shops and hotels. On the west of the road, the houses and terraces are piled steeply against the slope of a hill, one street almost over-lapping another like slates on a roof. On the east, the side-roads slope down to the river. Everywhere the old houses were once packed tightly together as if space were as precious among the empty moors of Westmorland as on the island of New York. Sometimes, as you step further away from the main road and the light, you find a whole terrace opening on to a cobbled pavement only a few yards wide, where the houses are deserted and the doors and windows boarded up. At others you will find rubble or clear-ings as the old slums are pulled down and shovelled away. It has been suggested that these courts and alleys might have been patched up and preserved and turned into a street behind the street, an archaic arcade of tucked-away shops and showrooms to attract the tourist like the Rows at Chester. Compared with this, demolition is probably the more honourable fate, though I hope that the town will manage to hold on to at least some of the in-structive and heart-stirring ugliness of its past.

Yet the really important thing about Kendal—important not

just for itself but for the whole of the southern Lake District—
is that it is still alive in the present. It lies on the most popular
approach route to the Lakes, only about seven miles from Windermere, so that there are plenty of antique shops, gift shops,
cafés and hotels that cater for the tourist, though he is not allowed
to feel that he owns the town. The grocery and hardware stores
and the other shops still take the first place. If all the visitors
packed up and decided to go to the Channel Islands for their
holidays, Kendal, one feels sure, would be able to carry on.

For there is a fine independence about the town. It does not
need to be coddled or put into pickle. It can hold its own in the
scramble of modern industry and does not have to beg its living
from the pockets of London and Manchester. And to my mind,
such firm-based, local industry gives far better protection to the
life and integrity of the district than the guardianship of the
National Park Committee, necessary as this may be. For at Kendal
and the smaller market towns the industrial tradition of the Lakes
is still active, producing an honest living for the people without
turning them all into travel guides and museum curators.

Of these smaller market towns, Whitehaven, Egremont and
Millom are now completely absorbed into industrial West
Cumberland, while Appleby and Kirkby Lonsdale are almost
entirely rural. But Cockermouth, Penrith, Ulverston and, further
away, Wigton and Aspatria are all places where new or revived
industries are giving the Cumbrian and North Lancastrian a chance
to kick back.

I will glance at three of them—all quite handsome and just inside the main tourist area. Cockermouth is Wordsworth's town,
and the eighteenth-century house of Lord Lonsdale's unpaid
agent is still, apart from the castle, its most consequential edifice.
The main street has a spaciousness rare in Cumberland, though
the little side-streets are as packed as those of Kendal. With the
Derwent from Bassenthwaite and the Cocker from Crummock
both flowing into it, it is only a salmon-leap from the fells, yet
it belongs more with the industrial towns of the coast. The very
limestone of which most of it is built is the rock which bears the
iron ore of Egremont and Cleator Moor. There are factories
hidden away behind the narrow streets and many of the people
owe their living to the new prosperity of Whitehaven and
Workington. Even the speech in the streets and shops is tuned to

the dialect of industrial Cumberland rather than to that of the dales, and this, to some extent, is true of Keswick also.

Penrith and Ulverston both lie further away from West Cumberland, though Ulverston once shared in the iron industry which is now concentrated at Barrow. Penrith is the chief of the sandstone towns, looking north to the Eden Plain and the old Forest of Inglewood. It is a red, solid town, comfortable as a farm-house kitchen until the A6 began to jangle its chains along the streets. Ulverston, on the other hand, is grey and white, built on the junction of the slate and the limestone, between the Morecambe Bay valleys and Low Furness. Both towns take much from the eighteenth century. Penrith—even in its parish church—has the look of that prosperous, self-righteous, Age-of-Reason Dissent which the young Wordsworth hated; while Ulverston has more of the elegance of the time, being a kind of minor north-country spa, without the waters, where gentry came for the theatre and for dances. Each town is dominated by a hill. At Penrith it is the Beacon, now partly occupied by both the living and the dead, though its top still has something of the "visionary dreariness" with which Wordsworth painted it.[1] And at Ulverston it is the Hoad, more detached than the Beacon though not more rugged. It looks across the salt marshes and sands of the Bay and carries a monument in the form of a lighthouse that makes it look like a town-crier's bell standing, mouth-downwards, with the handle sticking up in the air. (The lighthouse is dedicated to the memory of Sir John Barrow, born at Ulverston in 1764, who became a high official of the Admiralty, and in 1831 published the story of *The Mutiny of the Bounty*. Fletcher Christian, the leader of the mutineers, was himself a Cumbrian, born near Cockermouth and educated at the local grammar school where, for a time, William Wordsworth must have been a fellow pupil.[2]) In the nineteenth century Ulverston had important blast furnaces, but these are now demolished and a penicillin factory has been set up in their place. The whole of this section of Morecambe Bay is almost astonishingly unsullied and unspoilt in spite of the fact that industry of one type or another has been carried on there since at least the early Middle Ages.

[1] *The Prelude:* Book XII, lines 225-69.
[2] See: C. S. Wilkinson: *The Wake of the Bounty* (1953), for a highly entertaining speculation on a possible association between Christian and Wordsworth.

One other town remains to be mentioned—Barrow-in-Furness. Historically, it does not belong to the Lake District at all. In the eighteenth century, when Whitehaven was already a thriving sea-port, and there were small but busy iron-works in nearly all the valleys of Low Furness, Barrow did not exist even as a village. Not until the 1840s was it planned into existence by Ramsden and Schneider and the Dukes of Devonshire and Buccleuch on the extreme tip of a long peninsula so far from the fells as to be scarcely aware of them. With the coming of the railway and the lake steamers a day trip to Windermere or Coniston became possible for most Barrow people but it was still a trip into what seemed a foreign country.

Today this is changed. The population has not grown very much in recent years and because of the nature of the ship-building trade it is not very likely to grow. But the town has now absorbed nearly the whole of the industry of Askam, Lindal, Dalton and the rest of Low Furness, and is the one great centre of employment in the area. More and more, the villages within about ten miles of Walney Channel are coming to depend on Barrow. Like Kendal—though without Kendal's five-hundred-year training for the job—it is becoming the half-reluctant god-father of a large section of the Lake country.

The town itself, with the high tide on three sides of it and the winds from Ireland all over and through it, is surely the cleanest of all towns in the north of England engaged in heavy industry. It was planned on the grid-system, with the roads meeting at right angles—the main one being as wide as a football pitch with trees along the touch-line. There is little of the tang of the sea-port in any of this. But in the older streets of the town, built partly on an island in the Channel, the salt has thoroughly soaked into the brick, and the masts and funnels of vessels, in dock or on the stocks, spike up above the backyard walls. There is a hundred-year-old theatre; there is a town hall as gothic as Grimm. And over the whole lot rises a cat's-cradle of cranes and derricks, which, on a late winter afternoon, tangles up the last red threads of the sunset.

IX

SPORT AND PASTIMES

How much of the present manner of life in the dales has been inherited from the Norsemen? Apart from the dialect there seems to be very little. I am not now thinking of the folk dances and ceremonies preserved with desperate enthusiasm in the way in which ornithologists protect a bird that is nearly extinct. Such survivals—the rush-bearing service at Grasmere and the proclamation of the Lammas Fair at the Market Place in Broughton-in-Furness[1] —are interesting and charming, though some of the daffodil and snowdrop rituals are about as antique as a hand-embroidered crinoline tea-cosy. But these, quite clearly, have little to do with the stuff of life: they appeal far more to the holiday-maker than to the local people. Nor, apart from swill-making, have the Lakes many local crafts to boast of.

Yet, though this may be merely a romantic self-deception, I think something of the spirit of the old Vikings lives on in the dalesman's love of sports. Of course, these, too, attract the visitor as well as the locals, and even as long ago as the time of Christopher North,[2] some of the greatest enthusiasts were to be found among off-comers. But in spite of the crowds at the more popular meetings, in spite of the publicity and tourist ballyhoo, the dale sports remain, at bottom, the dalesman's own business.

Fox-Hunting

Most of the dalesmen love hunting better than marriage, but, for my own part, I cannot pretend to speak of it with any enthusiasm. The Docetist heresy held that Our Lord did not really live and suffer on earth but only seemed to do so for the edification of the faithful. If it were possible to hold similar beliefs about the fox, then perhaps I could look on the hunt as one of the most exhilarating sports in the world, played on a superb sports ground. As it is, when the hounds stream across open fellside or nose up

[1] On the 1st August. The ceremony is marked by the distribution of coppers to the children but no fair is now held.

[2] I.e. John Wilson (1785–1854), professor of Moral Philosophy at Edinburgh.

and down a larch wood with a flurry of terriers behind them, I cannot forget a wretched animal with its lungs and heart half-burst even before the teeth get at it.

Nevertheless, in Cumberland hunting is not just a social gathering for organized cruelty. Foxes have to be kept down somehow and it is at least arguable that hunting is the most practical way of doing so. Anyway, the graces and snobberies of county society have little to do with the fell hunts.[1] The professional huntsman may wear the red coat[2] but his followers turn out in whatever will stand up best to the weather. For the hunting has to be done on foot, and as the fell foxes mostly lie well above the plough-line and nearly always make for the tops when pursued, the followers must be ready to face wind, rain and cold, to cross slopes shin-deep in bog or snow, or to go hours through mist, guessing where the hounds are from the sound of their voices. Many times both fox and hounds have fallen over precipices and dashed themselves to pieces.

The fox, whenever it can, will make for an earth or borran. Some of these are terrifying spots—chimneys or caves, plugged with chock-stones and rubble; or crumbling mountainsides where dumps of fallen boulders are riddled with holes and tunnels; or the abandoned workings of old mines and quarries where roof and walls are liable to cave in. This is where the terriers are needed. Their job is to enter the hole and make the fox bolt, but often they fight to the death in the dark cracks of the rock. Now and again neither fox nor dog emerges, and no amount of searching with crowbar or even dynamite can catch the one or save the other.

At other times the fox takes shelter on a "benk", a narrow ledge or cliff-face, where the hounds cannot reach it. Sometimes, after the hounds are called off, it cannot make its way back from its refuge and has to stay there till it starves or falls. There is a story of a man who was lowered on a rope to shift a fox from such a perch, and succeeded so well that the rest of the hunt went off excitedly, leaving the man dangling in mid-air.[3]

---

[1] I do not speak of the lowland hunts of which there are several.

[2] Cumberland people still argue as to whether John Peel wore a red coat or not. The evidence seems inconclusive, but for my own part I am satisfied that the "coat so gay" of the song was really a "coat so *grey*".

[3] See: Richard Clapham: *Fox hunting on the Lakeland Fells.*

Probably the best way to watch a hunt is to get well up among the fells before it begins. With any luck you may be able to view all the first part without moving more than a few yards, and if the fox gets well away you can follow on the level without having to climb. But the most popular method at present seems to be to follow by motor-car. When the fox strikes up the fellside, the followers set off along the narrow roads and farm tracks for that spot in the next valley where it is most likely to come down. Visitors with large cars who choose to drive along these roads in the opposite direction will have a good opportunity to study the dialect. Before long, no doubt, groups of Manchester sportsmen will be following the pack by helicopter.

There are five fell-packs—the Ullswater (hunting Patterdale and Mardale), the Blencathra (Skiddaw and Borrowdale,) the Mellbreak (Lorton, Buttermere, Loweswater), the Eskdale and Ennerdale (the western dales), and the Coniston (Old Man and Langdale). Of them all, the Eskdale and Ennerdale probably hunts the wildest and roughest country, including Pillar and Scafell. From these fells, even if a fox takes to the lowlands, it still faces hazardous country—the mosses and sands of Esk and Duddon, the dunes of the coast, or the iron-ore mines of Hodbarrow and Egremont, where the going is every bit as rough as on the fells.

When the hunt met at Hodbarrow Hollow, among the old tips and quarries, there were often so many foxes about that the hounds did not know which one they were chasing.

Because of "D'ye Ken John Peel", many people think of Cumberland as the typical hunting county, with Peel himself as the master of a fashionable hunt. But there was nothing fashionable about John Peel. He came, not from the gentry, but from ordinary farming stock, living at Caldbeck, and hunting the fells round about Skiddaw with his own small pack of hounds. This was rough work—out every morning at five or six o'clock, no horses (except for the pony on which he rode to the meet), and—unless I am wrong about the "coat so grey"—no red coats. Peel died in 1854, and it was not until some years later that the song became popular, by which time the tune had lost the dotted quavers which give a lilt to the verses in the original version. John Woodcock Graves, who wrote the words of the song, liked Cumberland so little that he emigrated to Tasmania in 1833. Followers of the

Eskdale and Ennerdale swear that, in any case, John Peel was not to be compared with Tommy Dobson.

Hound-Trailing

Hound trails show that the heritage of the dales can sometimes pass from the farmers to the workers of the industrial coast without losing any of its true dale character. Trails first became popular at the country sports-meetings and every agricultural show still runs one. Then they began to be held in the small towns on the edge of the fell district, and now trailing is wide-spread and well organized under an Association founded in 1906. During summer and autumn there are trails nearly every day in one spot or another, and the more successful dogs may go out two or three times a week. Form is followed very closely, with trailing-notes published each week in the local papers, while the leading hounds are listed in a championship table according to the number of wins and places. The sport ranges into Lancashire and Yorkshire, but the chief centres, apart for the Lakes, are in the industrial areas of West Cumberland and Furness.

It is, moreover, a democratic sport, drawing its followers from all the strata of local society. The leading hounds are valuable animals, but it is not beyond the means of a working man to buy a pup and rear it, and if the dog grows into a winner, it becomes the pet and mascot of the neighbourhood.

Trailing, no doubt, owes its popularity partly to the love of gambling, and there used to be heart-breaking tales, during the lean years, of miners who starved their children in order to feed dogs on eggs, cream and sherry. But it seems likely that trailing also appeals to a scarcely understood backward-look at the old dale life. The delicious names given to the dogs seem to confirm this: Starlight, Lonning Lass, Lawless, Dowcrag, Briery, Fibre Mills.

Certainly a trail is often a grand sight—the hounds slipped in a field on the outskirts of the town to make their way across the farmland to the moors or fells which are never far off. Up they go to the tops, out of sight much of the time, and back again in thirty-five minutes or so. They have a curious leisurely way of running, taking wall and dyke in an easy-going stride and casting a friendly eye about them. The trail is laid by an aniseed mixture, dragged over the ground in an old sock. Two men start together from a point about mid-way round the course, and make their way, each by a different route, to the starting post. Many tricks were played in the past. False trails were laid down; hounds were lured off the course and fed or given drugs to make them thirsty; some were seized, carried off by car, and put back on the trail ahead of the others. Today there is much closer supervision, and most of the trails are well watched and guarded.

In recent years there has been a marked revival of another traditional sport of the mining towns—that of whippet-racing—and well-groomed, well-starved whippets, paraded like prize babies, are often seen in the streets. There was also an attempt, just after the War, to revive brass-putting, an old West Cumberland game, on the same principle as bowls, in which a heavy brass disk is pitched after a smaller jack. This is an after-work or out-of-work game of the waste lot, the scruffy green outside the public house where the geese wander and the children pile their bonfires in November. The revival seemed to come out of that spirit of neighbourliness shown in the Victory street parties of 1945, but, after a year or two, it dwindled away. Like quoits, brass-putting brought with it too much of the smell of the poverty years to appeal to the men of the new prosperity.

The Dale Sports

Hound trails are now one of the chief attractions at nearly all the dale sports. These may vary from village fruit and flower shows to popular meetings that draw crowds from all over the North West. The Travelling Bank attends the larger shows, and ice-cream vans and tricycles roll up from the towns, with horse-boxes for the increasingly popular horse and pony jumping. The local brass band bellows like a musical farm-yard, and the sound swells and fades in the wind with the smell of hawthorns and hay. Looking down from the tops, you see the crowd like wood-lice around the ring, and the marquee with its red pennons, and the cars lined up about the field. At one time these shows were favourites with all the young people from the smaller towns, but today it is probably only the dance in the evening which attracts many of the town folk. Yet the boys of the town still know how to get into the field behind the gate-keeper's back and are always ready to help to drive the animals from any one spot to any other. When I was a boy all the Millom schools were given a holiday for Green

Show,[1] held three miles away. Some of the mining towns have their own sports, such as Egremont Crab Fair, with dancing in the streets, a Fair Queen, and, at one time, a gurning competition.

Gurning—a sport which, alas, is in decline—consists of putting one's head through a horse-collar and pulling the ugliest face possible. And it was my privilege to know for many years one of the champion gurners of West Cumberland, of whom it was said that he had once won a competition without knowing that he had entered. He had merely been following the efforts of the other competitors with interest and sympathy.

Grasmere is the greatest of all the meetings, in its cup-like valley with the dark green of late summer slumping heavily on the woods and hills. It is held on the Thursday nearest 20th August—often one of the wettest times of the year in the Lakes—so that sometimes the valley is swimming with water the day before, and then, in the morning of the sports, the sky clears and the sun clamps down on the meadows like a red-hot plate. Or perhaps there is that warm, pewter-coloured haze, when the clouds are low, the fells flat as wood engravings, and there are hardly any shadows.

Whatever the weather, it cannot discourage the older dale folk to whom the sports are a passion. I knew one old man who, as a youth in the 1870s, lived just below Boot in Eskdale. He worked on the Irton estates, and after his day's work would meet his friends at The Woolpack Inn a mile above Boot village. It was the eve of Grasmere Sports, and half a dozen of them decided to go. They each went home, had supper and packed a few slices of bread, and then met again at "The Woolpack". They set off over Hardknott —then, of course, only a rough, pony-track—to Cockley Beck and over Wrynose into Little Langdale. It was midnight when they reached "The Tourist's Rest"[2] in the village, but one of them knew the landlord and persuaded him to let them sleep on the kitchen floor. After breakfast they went by Elterwater and Red Bank to Grasmere, watched the sports, came back the same fourteen or fifteen miles overnight, and were at work the next morning. The old man remembered every yard of that journey and almost every bout of the wrestling. Yet, in spite of his love of the dales,

---

[1] The annual show of Millom and Broughton Agricultural Society, now no longer held at The Green, but still known as "Green Show".
[2] Now re-named The Three Shires Inn.

the need to find work had drawn him away from them. First of all he got a job helping to build the Eskdale railway. He would tell how the men made use of the gangers' wagon to have a night out at Ravenglass—free-wheeling downhill and pumping themselves slowly back again. Then he became a miner—first at Eskdale, then at the little mines at Kirksanton, south of Black Combe, and finally at Hodbarrow. He was very old when I knew him, and would walk slowly along the asphalted footpath beside the slag-banks of the Duddon Estuary, with the fells among which he was born standing out on the sky-line.

The most spectacular event in dale sport is undoubtedly the Guides' Race. The route is always out of the field to the steepest slope nearby, up for fifteen hundred feet or so, and down again, Not all dale sports are conveniently situated for such a race, but at Grasmere and Coniston the whole fellside becomes a magnificent stadium, with an obstacle course of crags, screes, grass rakes and sheep trods, with spikings of rowan, holly, birch and juniper. The competitors walk, run, climb or scramble up as best they can, but once they are at the top, the nature of the race changes, for they come down in a kangaroo chain of leaps, jumping from crag to crag, crashing through the bushes, glissading down the screes. A man who reaches the turn with a lead of twenty yards is likely to be a hundred yards ahead less than a minute later.

Wrestling

But it is the wrestling which really holds the heart of the Cumbrian.

Wrestling, in the Cumberland and Westmorland style, is the most good-natured of all forms of physical combat. It needs a calm concentration and watchfulness which leaves no place for malice or anger. If you lose your temper you will probably lose the fall. Often you will see men smiling quietly to themselves as they waltz round one another, waiting for a chance to attack, and when they fall they get up with the look of surprise that you see on the face of a very young child who knows that he cannot walk without falling but is never quite ready for the fall when it comes.

The men stand face to face, breast to breast, locked closer than lovers, each clasping hands behind the other's back, one arm above a shoulder and one below. If a man breaks hold, except when throwing his opponent, he loses the fall. The round ends when a man is down—there is no need for both shoulders to be touching the ground as in some forms of wrestling. Usually both men fall together, and the loser is the one who is below. Sometimes a skilful and agile wrestler can twist in the arms of an opponent even as he is being thrown and so end the fall uppermost. Physical strength alone is not so important as may be thought. A man who is much the stronger of the two can always win by forcing in his opponent's back, but granted that there is a reasonable balance of weight and stature, the fall will usually go to the more skilful or more enterprising wrestler.

Of the methods of attack—hipeing, inside striking, in and out, the chip, haming, hankering the heel, haunching, cross-buttocking and the like—I will not presume to speak. The terms would mean nothing to those who have not themselves tried to wrestle—not even as boys at school—and indeed, the majority of the spectators at the big meetings know little of the techniques they are watching. Dale wrestling is really a sport for the wrestler, not the spectator. It is a standard joke that if you want to see the wrestling at Grasmere you have to enter for it. This is true in more than the obvious sense. For all the spectator gets is a sight of two men staggering round one another like a couple of drunks trying to dance. The real contest is lost to him. It is not to be *seen* at all. To appreciate wrestling the mind must think in images which are largely tactile. The wrestler must fix his hold, keep his balance, and try to read the mind of his opponent entirely by touch. It is a sport for individualists; for men who want to be in it; for men who like a laal furtle.

We hear of wrestling in Cumberland as early as the seventeenth century, but the first organized meetings seem to have been Melmerby Rounds on Midsummer Day and Langwathy Rounds on New Year's Day, both of which were well established by the end' of the eighteenth century. Another meeting was held in July at the top of High Street in the Ullswater Fells, where the wrestlers would have to wait for their second wind before beginning the contest. In the early nineteenth century Professor Wilson ("Christopher North") helped to set up the sport at Ambleside, after which Keswick rose in importance as a wrestling centre. Finally the "metropolitan" competitions were organized at Carlisle, the winner of which might call himself World Champion, Cumberland and Westmorland style.

We now come to a magnificent list of names which have in them the bone and breed of the dales: William Richardson of Caldbeck, Thos. Nicholson of Threlkeld, Miles and James Dixon, Harry Graham of Brigham, Robert Rowantree, William Dickinson, Tom Todd, the Rev. Abraham Brown, and many more, almost forgotten, such as those given by William Litt: ". . . . his last four opponents being A. Armstrong, J. Frears, T. Richardson, and T. Lock, all of them good wrestlers".[1] Litt himself was a good wrestler, too, and in 1811 met Harry Graham on Arlecdon Moor for a purse of sixty guineas—the largest sum wrestled for up to that date. But his fame—if we can speak of the fame of one whose name is known only to Cumbrians and not so many of them— depends not on his own prowess but on the fame he gave to others. For *Wrestliana*, his account of the early wrestling and wrestlers, is one of the classics of the literature of sport, worthy to go beside John Nyren's *Young Cricketer's Tutor*.

After Litt's time the wrestling grew even more popular, until in 1851 a championship match was held at Flan How, Ulverston, for a purse of £300. Then, in the latter half of the century, Grasmere became the capital of the wrestling world, dominated by the figure of George Steadman, heavyweight champion for thirty years—a massive man of over eighteen stone in his prime. Steadman's last appearance in the ring was at the age of fifty-four, in 1900, when he defeated Hexham Clarke in the final at Grasmere. Four years later he died at Brough. In photographs he looks calm and almost benign, with a huge forehead and white side-whiskers like those of a Victorian archdeacon, but the strength of the man shows in the waves of muscles along his forearm and the link-like lock of fingers on fingers. He wore the traditional costume—still worn today—of white underpants, white vest and embroidered drawers, and, of course, he wrestled in stocking feet. Steadman's son was also a well-known wrestler, and once broke the collar-bone of an uncle of mine—not, however, wrestling, but playing rugby. The most celebrated wrestler of post-war years is Ted Dunglinson, who has won the Grasmere heavyweight contest more often than any but Steadman. Dunglinson—who trained at Gilsland Wrestling Academy—attended

[1] William Litt: *Wrestliana* (Whitehaven, 1823).

Carlisle Grammar School and was at one time a chorister in the cathedral,[1] thereby showing that wrestlers need not be confined to the pupils of remote country schools. Indeed, I would like to see wrestling included in the physical training syllabus of every secondary school in the county, for it is an excellent, healthy, amiable sport, and one which we should not let die out if we can possibly help it.

Some New Sports

Even since the time of Professor Wilson there have been men who look on the Lakes as a gigantic gymnasium, where the visitor from the towns can find space and fresh air, and can test his skill, daring and endurance. I suppose it is the mere prejudice of one who has hated athletics since childhood which makes me detest this point of view. Too much of my youth had to be spent trying to save my life for me to see much fun in risking it on rocks or in water. Others disagree, however, and rock-climbing, skin-diving and the gentler art of sailing have become very popular in recent years. All three, of course, are holiday pastimes, appealing more to the visitor than the local man, though they now have many followers among the scientists and technicians of the newer industries.

For the marathon walkers and record breakers, I can raise nothing but a kind of bewildered grin—the two Grasmere men, for instance, who claim to have swum in every one of the district's four hundred and sixty-three tarns; or the Heaton brothers, from East Lancashire, one of whom, in 1961, climbed fifty-one Lake peaks in twenty-four hours, while, a year later, the other climbed fifty-four.[2]

Many of these men have a real love of the rocks and some of them have a practical knowledge which I can only envy. And none

---

[1] See: A. H. Griffin: *Inside the Real Lakeland* (Guardian Press, 1961).

[2] "His route from Keswick was up Skiddaw, Great Calva, and Blencathra to Threlkeld, where they (i.e. the two brothers) arrived more than one hour ahead of schedule, and Dodds, the Helvellyn Range, Fairfield right to Langdale. After that came Pike o' Blisco, Crinkle Crags, Bowfell, and all the Scafell range to Wasdale Head, which they reached behind time. Then the Pillar and Gable fells to Honister, the Dale Head–Hindscarth–Robinson ridge, and, finally, the additional fells of Aiken Knott, Scar Crag and Causey Pike, and the long run back to Keswick." *Manchester Guardian.*

of them, in any case, interferes with my own enjoyment or with that of anybody else.

But this can scarcely be said for the speed-boaters, the water-skiers, or the organizers of motor rallies, motor-cycle scrambles and go-kart races, all of which bring turmoil, noise and stink to the very spots where one goes primarily to escape them. To ban such things is not to be autocratic but merely to help the National Park to carry out the purpose for which it was established. What is the point of preserving the Lake shores pure and unsullied to the eye if they are allowed to sound and smell like a factory-town bus-station with a juke-box and pin-table saloon next door?

Pooley Bridge

X

THE MINING SCENE

Mining in the Fells

MINING has a long history in the Lake District. The Celtic tribes dug for copper. The Romans knew of the presence of copper, lead, zinc, iron and silver. By the end of the sixteenth century German miners were well established at Keswick, and furnaces were smelting ore mostly from the mines of Newlands, but also from Caldbeck and Coniston. Elizabethan Keswick was a busy, cosmopolitan industrial town, noisy with quarrels in three languages and with brawls between Cumbrian and foreign workmen until the latter married Cumberland girls and became Cumbrians themselves.

The main ores of the district were copper, haematite, blende (producing zinc) and galena (lead)—the latter having often been rich in silver, while the Goldscope Mine in Newlands has produced some gold. Lead alone has been of any importance in recent years, and there was some post-war development at the Greenside mine at Glenridding, though this was finally closed down in 1961, after having been used during the previous year by the Atomic Energy Authority for experiments in the detection of underground explosions. Commercially the most important deposit still being worked in the inner Lake area is not a metal ore but the diatomite in the bed of a former lake at Kentmere—a deposit composed of the remains of the minute water-plants called diatoms. Barytes or heavy spar (sulphate of barium) has also been obtained in recent years from a number of small mines, mostly in the Caldbeck Fells and at Force Crag at the head of Coledale near Braithwaite, but this, too, seems to be in decline.

Before the invention of gunpowder, mining was a very difficult operation. The miners of those times—almost mythically called "The Old Men"—worked like explorers in the dark, cutting openings just big enough to get through, prospecting for themselves, and in some cases raising ore on their own account and paying only a "tribute" to the landowner. Local folk-lore is full of stories of miners who found rich deposits of ore, revealed to them by the fairies or the devil. Sometimes they made secret little hoards in a cave or tunnel, saving up for their old age, and then perhaps died before they drew out the balance, leaving it for future generations to find.

The Iron Mines

The fell mines belong to the romantic past, but the iron mines of the coast are the foundation of modern Cumberland, even though, today, they are almost all derelict.

Oddly enough, it was among the fells that iron seems first to have been found: in Ennerdale, Eskdale, Dunnerdale and High Furness. There are signs of early smelting—patches of slag or cinders—in Eskdale, Wasdale and around Coniston Lake. Then, in the Middle Ages, the mining of iron ore increased considerably around Egremont, where it has gone on more or less continuously ever since.

It was in Lancashire, however, among the Furness Fells, that the industry developed on a larger scale, with charcoal from the woods used for the firing. Often the bloomery was set up in a narrow gorge beside a beck, where the wind would sweep down and supply blast without bellows. During the sixteenth century, Coniston and Hawkshead must have been centres of a little Black Country, with charcoal-burners living in their huts in the woods, and the smoke of the furnaces drifting up above the trees. Some of the Furness trade crossed the Duddon to Millom, where the Huddlestons of Millom Castle set up a bloomery to smelt the ore mined nearby at Water Blean. When the Water Blean supply failed they seem to have imported a certain amount of ore, being quite unaware that at Hodbarrow Mains—the outlying part of their estate—there was waiting one of the richest deposits in the whole world.

The early eighteenth century brought the cold blast-furnace which led to the modern period. In 1711, the first of these furnaces was built at Backbarrow, and was followed by half a dozen or more in Furness, one at Duddon Bridge, and a group at Maryport, Frizington and other places on the edge of the Cumberland coalfield. The Duddon Furnace, which was working until 1880, still stands in the riverside woods, looking like a ruined church or monastic barn, with waterfalls of ferns splashing down its walls and a reek of ramsons about it like an ironic incense.

The great Cumberland and North Lancashire iron industry of the nineteenth century grouped itself round the two main ore-producing areas, both of which occur in the western curve of the limestone that encircles the fells. The larger of the two lies in a narrow band between the Skiddaw slates of lower Ennerdale and the coal measures of Whitehaven-Workington. It starts about Beckermet and continues through Cleator, Cleator Moor, Frizington and Rowrah to about Lamplugh. At one of the mines at Montreal, Cleator Moor, iron and coal were at one time raised from the same shaft. The second ore-producing area is mainly in Furness, around Dalton, Lindal and Askam, though it appears also on the Cumberland side of the Duddon at Millom and Kirksanton. The total production of the West Cumberland district was the greater of the two, but Hodbarrow, Millom, much exceeded any other mine during the years of its maximum output. The prosperity of the mines grew enormously in the second half of the nineteenth century because of the opening of local blast-furnaces, but it began to decline in West Cumberland after 1890, though Hodbarrow continued to expand until the beginning of this century. Since then the output has steadily fallen away. All the mines in Furness have been closed for a good many years; Hodbarrow finally closed in 1968; and only one small mine is still working in West Cumberland, supplying ore to Workington. Such is inevitable, since mining always exhausts. Today very few people in Cumberland depend for their living on the production of iron-ore, yet it is the iron which gave us our towns, our streets, our chapels, and the tone and bone of our society. Modern Cumberland may earn its keep from silk, leather, nylons, berets and soapless detergents, but, like a glass and concrete skyscraper, its inner structure is of iron.

In many ways mining has much in common with agriculture, and iron-ore mining, in particular, remains a kind of rural industry. To begin with, the mines are mostly small and do not wither and scarify great tracts of the landscape. Then, also, there is a surprising freedom from dirt. The soil around the mines is rich and red, and the red dust soaks into the wood of fences and railway sleepers, staining them to mahogany, while pools, drains and becks run red as blood. Where there are new workings, the tips and rubble heaps are a raw, arterial red, as if the earth had been coughing up its lungs. But as soon as the workings are closed down, the scars begin to heal and the redness is whiskered over with horse-tails and rough grasses.

In the Furness area, most of the mines have been closed for half a century—the last closed down thirty years ago—so that by now they have already been re-assimilated into the country scene. The broken-down mine buildings, or what is left of them, are all built of the white limestone, like the field walls and the barns, and there are huge feather-boas of ivy flopping round the windows. The old shafts are stuffed to the gullet with hawthorns and elders, and often the land has caved in round about, till it looks like a lump of red clay, punched and pitted with hollows and holes. Around St. Helen's level crossing, on the railway line between Barrow and Askam, and again at Roan Head on the estuary, there are enormous quarried-out pits and basins, plug-full with water, standing like tarns, with shores of hacked red-and-white limestone and deltas of gravel.

Further north, in West Cumberland, where some mines are still at work, the landscape is more obviously industrial. The ground here is by nature rough and knobbly, and this has been emphasized and copied by the artificial hills of tips and slag-banks and the artificial combes of subsidences. It is not so rich a landscape as that of Furness and the limestone rarely forces itself on your notice. On the one side, dull, dirty moors decline to the colliery coast, and on the other, the bare hills of the Skiddaw Slate heave up towards Ennerdale. Even the towns seem to have ignored the limestone and to have turned, instead, to the easily-obtained red sandstone of St. Bees. Nearly all the mines are now abandoned but you cannot forget them, as you can in Furness, for mines and towns are so close together.

There is a new prosperity in the towns now, but the corpse of their old prosperity lies unburied at the back-door—bones splintered, limbs half-gnawed away, bowels dragged out and left to dry in the sun.

At the southern tip of the county, at Millom, where the iron emerges on the coast, the landscape takes on a salty taste, and the limestone is yellowed and gritted with sand. The magnificent Hodbarrow Mines are the foundation stone of the town in which I was born—though, oddly enough, that stone (i.e. limestone) does not show itself anywhere in the streets, for the houses are built almost entirely of slate. The mines lie a mile or so away on the promontory which acts as the southern kerbstone of Cumberland county. The first shaft was sunk at Towsey Hole, at the exact point where the rocks grapple with the tide. It is still there, choked with bramble and thorn, among ledges heaped with rock-roses and bloody cranesbill. When I was a boy my dog chased a rabbit and fell down the shaft, to crawl out again, cut and bruised but otherwise unhurt. Nearby is a ruined windmill, used as an office in the early days of the mine, and not far away is the first lighthouse, built on the limestone pavement—as full of fossils as Cumberland cake is full of currants—which shelves down to what was then the shore.

But as more ore was detected, that shore was slowly pushed backwards. A sea-wall was built to keep out the high tide, and, later, when ore was discovered beneath the sea, another wall was thrown out in a great arc of a mile and a quarter stretching from Hodbarrow Point to Haverigg. Finally the older wall cracked and collapsed like the Great Wall of China as the land caved in over the abandoned workings.

Between the old and the new walls lay a new parish—one of the wildest and emptiest in Cumberland. To the south it is cut off from the sea by the rim of the new barrier. To the north it is cut off from the town by the steep slope of the former shore-line. The old pit-heads stand above an escarpment of sand and ore, with two brick towers looking like the west end of a Norman cathedral. From shaft to shaft there is a spider-webbing of broken girders, chutes, loading gear, pylons and telephone wires. The sleepers of the little railways, with the lines torn off for scrap, run up and down the slopes like the Big Dipper at Blackpool. For all its present emptiness, Hodbarrow still looks a busy, fussy spot—a rock landscape as challenging as that of Great Langdale.

But down in the hollow between the walls you used to be in a landscape as peaceful as any among the highest fells. The old swash channel runs across the sand like a dried-up wadi in a desert. Terns, gulls and oyster-catchers nest among the stones. Dwarf willows are pegged to the ground like circular mats for some giant to rest his beer-mug on, and there is sea-spurge, sea-holly and marram grass, and, where the sand is damper, there are scruffles of blackberry and the rarer dewberry. An old ore-bogie lies upended beside a rabbit's skeleton, and a railway sleeper is pickled, half-petrified, in the salt. It looks like a landscape of antiquity, a Valley of Dry Bones, yet it is scarcely sixty years old and will certainly not last another sixty years. For, with the closing of the mines the pumps stopped working, and since then the hollow has slowly filled with water. Month by month a new inland lake has been rising and spreading, and future generations will no longer be able to stand below sea-level and look up through the pit-heads to the top of Scafell Pike, eighteen miles away—the highest and the lowest bench-marks in all Cumberland seen in one single sweep of the eye.

Blast-Furnaces

The modern haematite pig-iron industry did not begin in Cumberland until the middle of the last century. In 1841 blast-furnaces were opened at Cleator Moor—a strange town, which sprang out of the bare rock into sudden prosperity and remained, chained to the rock like Andromeda, long after that prosperity had been blasted away. In the next decade furnaces were set up at Seaton, Harrington and Workington, and (in Lancashire) at Barrow. The trade expanded in the sixties and seventies, spreading to Distington and Maryport in West Cumberland, to Millom in the south, and to Ulverston and Askam in Furness. Today, it is concentrated at Workington and Barrow, though with enormously increased production.

Workington and Barrow have become large industrial towns, standing rather apart from the fells. Millom retained to the end the smaller scale of the nineteenth-century furnace, and stood within shouting distance of the western fells, the last conspicuous sign of a two-thousand-year-old industry.

There can be no argument about its conspicuousness, at any rate. The works were sited on a peninsula which almost shuts up the mouth of the Duddon. At high tide they advance into the middle of a sea-loch, and from the hills across the estuary—from Gaw-thwaite or Kirkby Moors—they look like a huge battle-ship sailing out with all funnels smoking. They are visible from Scafell, Scafell Pike, Great End, Harter Fell in Eskdale, Crinkle Crags, Bowfell, Grey Friar, Dow Crag, Coniston Old Man, and from some points on Kirkstone. Seen from the hills between Broughton and Coniston, they make a fine, swinging climax to the estuary, trombones, tubas and euphoniums marching out at full blare. If the oak-woods are what the botanists and ecologists call the "climax" vegetation of the dales, then these iron-works were the "climax" industry of the coast.

But, as with the oak-woods, it is a climax which has been passed. For the method of producing steel from iron-ore by the intermediate process of pig-iron is gradually being superseded, and the Millom Ironworks were closed down in October, 1968, bringing heavy unemployment to a town which had relied on iron for a hundred years. Today the empty shell of the old furnaces and the un-smoking chimney stacks have a pathetically archaic look about them. Small, isolated, blasting defiance at the fells, they belong to the Heroic Age of Lake industry.

Iron-smelting, unfortunately, is not all heroics, for around the furnaces lie the grave-yards of the murdered rock. There is a repulsiveness about slag-banks.[1] It cannot be because of their colour, since they are the colour of stone. It cannot be because of their shape, since they are more or less the shape of tumuli or alluvial hills. It cannot even be because of dirt, since slag is freer from grime and fume than are most industrial excreta. It must be because slag is so dead. It does not alter with the seasons and scarcely alters with the years. It is empty of birds and even of rats. It scarcely shows any signs of decay. There are slag-banks abandoned forty or fifty years ago which are still bald and grey as a slate roof. They jag up above the backyard doors of some of the older terraced houses—a bleak cliff, as intimidating as the screes of Wastwater, bringing the greyness of November into almost every month of the year.

Yet on the top of a slag-bank, for all the dead, lava-like look of its pavement, there is a spaciousness and freedom not unlike that of the fell-tops. The boys run about as on the ramparts of a castle. There is nothing whatever that they can damage and scarcely anyone even to pretend to shoo them off. There are scars, slopes, dips, corries, hollows, caves and sometimes tunnels. It

---

[1] The term "slag-bank" is sometimes used incorrectly to include coal-tips, the spoil-heaps of mines and quarries, and the rubble-dumps of chemical and other industries. It is used here to mean the tips of dross separated in the reduction of ore.

is a place for ambushes and secret parleyings and all the frightening privacies of pre-adolescence. From the Millom slag-bank you can stare down into streets and backyards as from a camera obscura. Or you can look further, up the most magnificent estuarine view in the north of England, to the highest peaks of three counties. Unfortunately, in recent years, slag has been tipped as a flat plat-form on one of the sand-banks in the estuary itself. I have heard it said that the height of this platform has been restricted to make it less conspicuous. If that is true, then the decision was wrong. An old-fashioned slag-bank on the waste land behind the furnaces would have been far less of an eye-sore. As it is, the slag covers a much wider area than it need have done, while the estuary and the sea-shore for some miles around are being jetsammed with what looks like a shingle of pumice-stone.

Many of the smaller slag-banks, however, slope neither into the sea nor into the streets, but into meadows where buttercups and eyebright grow among the crumbles of slag, or into swamps and flashes full of Dutch rush and lesser spearwort. At Askam the old bank juts out into the estuary like a pier, making a great place for flook fishers. Here sand is beginning to upholster the slag, while in other places tippings of soil and ore-rubble have given the weeds a chance to shade a green crayon over the greyness. Else-where, slag has been dug out and carried away for road material, aerodrome foundations and the like. No doubt much more could have been done by tipping, planting and levelling to help the landscape re-assimilate the old slag-banks—though, for my part, I have no wish to see them neatly camouflaged with lawns and elders like disguised air-raid shelters in a municipal park.

At a distance they often need no camouflage at all. They can be gravely beautiful under snow and there are winter evenings when the sky is purple and the electric wires and thorn-trees are black and the slag-banks slant out of the mist, lonely as ice-bergs and mauve as partly cooked white of egg.

But it is at night that the slag flares into flamboyant beauty— the slag of the few still working furnaces. You watch the little engine climb the bank with the bogies behind it, dim in the smoke. The engine stops, pauses, runs forward again. The bogie swings over. For a moment the slag remains tilted, a burning moon looking straight at you—from a hundred yards away, you can still feel the heat on your face. Then the crust breaks and the red-hot syrup pours down the side of the bank. The light does not flash out, but spreads quickly across the sky as if a packet of red dye had been dipped in the night, and then ebbs away until there are only a few volcanic trickles glowing on the slope of the bank. And at high tide the slag floods the estuary with fire, and the lights of bank and furnace float out on the water, puckering and splintering on the burning waves.

The Coal Mines

Coal was known to the early Britons in Cumberland and to the Romans, but in their days wood and peat were preferred as fuel, and it was not until the early seventeenth century that outcrops began to be worked at Whitehaven. Round about that time the land which had formerly belonged to St. Bees Priory passed into the hands of the Lowther family, and under Sir Christopher Lowther, who settled in Whitehaven, and his son, Sir John, who succeeded him in 1644, the coal trade began to develop rapidly. A harbour was made in the creek, and by 1700 the Lowther pits were producing 27,000 tons of coal a year. Further north, the Curwen family began on a smaller scale at Workington. By the mid-eighteenth century Whitehaven was one of the three or four most important ports in England, shipping a large tonnage of coal to Ireland. For a time it seemed likely that the town would become one of the main centres of English trade with the New World, but its isolation, the emptiness of the country behind it and the difficulties of over-land communication were too great a handicap.

Nevertheless, the coal trade went on growing. More shafts were sunk and deeper ones, and soon it was realized that huge stocks of coal lay beneath the sea. At Whitehaven the workings stretch out about four miles from the shore at the furthest point and it has been estimated that the coal may extend outwards for another eight miles though it seems very unlikely that·it will be practicable or profitable to mine it. In fact, the difficulties and high cost of mining in Cumberland throw a doubt over the whole future of the coal-field. Already the Coal Board has closed down all but two or three mines.

But the cost of coal is not to be counted only in pounds per ton. The sea added great hazards. In the account books of the collieries we read of one accident after another. Men, boys, horses, and even women, who sometimes worked stripped to the waist beside the men, were trapped by falls of the roof or by the in-rush of water. In 1837, the sea broke into three Workington collieries, causing great loss of life; in 1910, 136 lives were lost in an explosion at Whitehaven; in 1947, 104 at William Pit in the same town.

The miner divided this coal-field into three sections—the area where the coal measures are exposed or covered only by boulder clay; the area of under-sea coal; and the area, to the north and south, where the coal seams dip under the sandstone of St. Bees and the Cumberland Plain. But to those who view the field from the surface it seems to fall into three different sections, according to the nature of the country. First, and by far the most important, there is the colliery coast, stretching from Whitehaven to Workington and on as far as Maryport. Secondly, a narrow whip of coal curving to the north-east of Maryport, as far as Aspatria, where it touches the edge of the old Inglewood Forest. And thirdly, the scattered group of villages, mostly well above sea-level, bordering the Egremont–Frizington iron-ore country.

It is this third section, alone among the three, which really belongs to the Lake area. As you mount the hill from Whitehaven, you come out on a high table-land, looking east to Ennerdale, west to the sea, and north to Scotland. The land is farmed, but it has the look of moorland. Plovers settle in the ploughed fields, and in the meadows there are patches of swamp and rocks. It is a bare, open landscape, lifted towards the sky. The fields have that soiled and cindery look which is always found near a colliery, but they still belong to the moorland and the curlews have not left them. From above Moresby you can see the coal haze hanging over the coast, but where the sunlight can get through it lies like a gilt lacquer on the black sea. The stone of walls and houses is of dark sandstone, but when the sun breathes on it you can rub up geranium colours from under the grime. In little dips and hollows you can find farms, cottages, country houses, even a theatre, all of sandstone, cosy as a tea-pot cover. But when you climb higher you see the smudges of coal across the face of the moor —little Coolins of slack, clinkery screes, abandoned pit-gear and railway lines. At Pica a whole train-load of miners' houses has been shunted into a siding, left there and forgotten. Down in the valley of the Ehen the black dirt of the coal and the red dirt of the iron-ore turn every privet and hawthorn into a blackberry bush. All the smaller mines are now closed, and the men of Moresby, Pica, Keekle, Moor Row, Lowca and Arlecdon work in the Whitehaven pits, or at Marchon or Windscale or at one of the new local factories. The sting of poverty has gone from the grime, but, apart from a coat of paint, these villages still look much as they did thirty years ago.

The colliery coast contains scenery more completely ravaged by industry than any other in Cumberland, but also more dramatic. Looking north from Kells, across the lobster-claws of Whitehaven harbour, you see the cliffs looping in and out in small bays and promontories as far as Workington. One colliery stands on the cliff top, the screes of coal sliding almost over the edge. Wagons used to be lowered on a wire rope down the steep slope to the harbour. The railway runs north on an embankment along the foot of the dark, purple cliffs, with patches of gorse and primroses among the rocks, and here and there buttresses of brick to prevent landslides from blocking the line. Below, the shore is a geological rubbish heap—massive fragments of sandstone, battered from the cliffs, flung about among shingle of coke and coal. In the depression of the twenties, when hills of coal stood unsold beside the pits, the miners and their wives would wander up and down the shore, filling sacks and buckets with drift-coal for their fires.

This is a landscape of almost Miltonic horror. There are old coke-ovens grown over with weed, columns of slag left stacked in the sea like strange Hebridean rocks, run-ways and mineral railways jutting out into the air like the prongs of broken forks, There are the old buildings of pits and workings—enormous sandstone halls, roofless and windowless, standing like ruined abbeys. And beside them are the miners' houses, many of them derelict, too—whole blocks caved in upon themselves. They crouch against the cliff with the rocks hanging over them like a thundercloud and the air in a perpetual drizzle of soot. The children paddle in the rock-pools, wiping the coal-dust off their feet as they dry them, and the boys play cricket on sandy pitches between the railway line and the slag.

This is not the Lake District as anyone thinks of it. Yet this is where the rocks of the fells bare their teeth for the last time, and two thousand years of mountain industry contemplate their

squalid aftermath. It is not only ironic, but historically and economically appropriate, that Borrowdale, Derwentwater, Bassenthwaite, Thirlmere (what Manchester doesn't want of it), Buttermere, Crummock, Loweswater and the Lorton Valley should
all empty their waters into the coal-blackened mud of Workington Harbour.

The Mining Towns

Whitehaven is no bigger than Workington but it is unquestion-
ably the capital of West Cumberland. It lies in a creek with the
double headland of St. Bees to the south, and to the east three hills
almost shouldering it into the sea. The town began with a well-
proportioned and spacious lay-out—attributed, according to
tradition, to Christopher Wren or one of his pupils—but soon
the space behind the comfortable main streets was packed with
courts and alleys, warehouses and slums. Today the slums are
being cleared away, as new housing estates spread along the
hills, but the town still holds on to its eighteenth-century look,
especially around the harbour. There is not much elegance about
it—though there are one or two handsome houses in Irish Street
and another, now the Town Hall, in Duke Street. Instead, it is
square, solid, plain to the point of rudeness—a style which typifies
all the money-mindedness, opportunism and single-vision of an
age that drove William Blake mad. Once there were shipping
offices, chandlers' shops, rope-makers, tallow-merchants, ships'
grocers and inns along the quay-side. Most of these are now
pulled down, but the few that are left, blotched with damp
though they may be, still have the shape and logic of their
period—window and door fitting into the wall as argument fits
into argument.

Whitehaven has no river and the shipping has to rely entirely
on the tides, so that fifty acres of sea have been fenced in by two
outer piers, while smaller piers divide the water-space into docks
and wharves. The piers themselves are great angular banks of
stone with neither wall nor handrail to prevent the drunks from
falling into the water. The west pier, the outer barrier of the harbour, ends with a lighthouse and a disposition of steps and corners
and blocks of masonry as formal as the entrance to a baroque
church. The heavy waves barge in through the harbour mouth
making the colliery coasters and trawlers and all the little rowing

boats rock like gulls. This is the world of Smollett and Rowland-
son without the laughs. Looking inward, you see the salty smoke
bronchially wheezing over the streets of the town, with church-
towers and factory-chimneys and row after row of sandstone
terraces and block after block of concrete council houses mounting
the hillsides to the moor-line. And flanking them, on either side,
are the scarred cliffs, scabbed with coal and blood. It is a landscape
as solemn as any in Cumberland.

The smaller industrial towns have none of this grandeur. For
the most part they were shovelled together in the nineteenth century of whatever building stone was handiest, and they remain
mean-looking, drab, ugly, haphazard in plan, yet mostly solid
enough to have stood up to a hundred years of west coast weather.
Many of them are little more than villages, with backyard doors
opening on to waste land and weeds, while Millom—the biggest
of the lot outside Whitehaven, Workington and Maryport—
has meadows and salt marshes pushing almost into the market
square. Harrington and Parton look out on the open sea; Askam-
in-Furness has dune-sand blowing up its streets; Rowrah and
Arlecdon take the full force of the wind from the Ennerdale fells.
Nowhere in England do countryside and industry come together
more closely or more poignantly.

These towns vary one from another more than do, say, those
of the Durham coalfield. They vary in the stone of which they
are built (sandstone, slate or limestone), in the industry from which
they were bred (coal, iron-ore or blast-furnace), and in the landscape in which they are set (sea-shore, estuary, valley or moor).
Yet they have one sombre characteristic in common. For until
about thirty years ago, they had all been in decline for nearly
half a century. Apart from a few semi-detacheds in the thirties
scarcely a house had been built since the death of Queen Victoria.
They remained chronically old-fashioned, shabby, botched-up
and nearly bankrupt. During the Depression those towns which
depended entirely on one blast-furnace or one mine shrivelled
into a kind of mummified despair. They felt that they were on the
very end of a dying branch of the economy, forgotten and ignored.
A whole generation of children was born, brought up, schooled,
half-fed and half-clothed on the dole, with hopes that rarely
reached out beyond the back-street or the slag-bank. Those who
were bright enough to get to the grammar school looked on this

as a way to escape from the town, and, but for the grace of God and the tubercle bacillus, I would have been one of them. It is easy to say that this is all over and done with. But the Depression is as much part of our history as the Roman Occupation or the coming of the Norsemen, and the memory of those times has marked the mind of every West Cumbrian over the age of fifty. It has marked the towns, too, for in spite of new shop fronts and bus shelters and television aerials, they seem not yet to have been dragged out of the nineteenth century. The nonconformist chapels thrust out square, fundamentalist chins against the mid-Victorian vices, and thousands of children are taught in buildings which still have the half-monastic, half-orphanage look of the old board school. The new housing estates stand rather outside the towns, not wholly integrated with them, looking as if they had been intended for Sheffield or Newcastle and had somehow slipped off the back of the lorry. Among the old, working-class terraces there are now bathrooms in the back-bedrooms and glass-and-veneer doors at the front, while door-posts, window-sills and gable-ends have been painted all the colours of the bill-posters. In the Ehen Valley in particular the once dark sandstone houses look as if they have been remodelled in plastic kitchenware. Yet these seem just off-comes and accidents, and the town's true character still proclaims itself in the Victorian three-storey terraces, with dormer-windowed attics, or the Boer war "khaki" houses, with free-stone facings and carpet-size gardens of pebble paths, Japanese anemones and hart's-tongue ferns.

Isolation has been a main part of the problem of these towns, but in the days of their first prosperity it was part of their pride. In the sixties and seventies miners flocked to West Cumberland from Cornwall and Wales and labourers came from Ireland. The county seemed to have been re-colonized by the Celts who had been driven away a thousand years before. They saw towns spring up out of nothing in five years and treble their size in ten. They felt themselves to be pioneers and adventurers, miles away from anywhere, cut off from the rest of the British Empire by the fells and the sea. So that in each town there developed an in-grown, independent society, stung and split by jealousies and class suspicion but banded together against the stranger like a clan. Every man, whatever his standing, depended on the one local industry as the men of a primitive village depended on the harvest. Generations—"all in the same boat"—grew up, married, quarrelled, competed against and relied upon one another, and the rest of the world seemed out of sight beyond the horizon.

For all this, each separate boat-load was a highly respectable fraternity. The Calvinism of the Welsh and the Methodism of the Cornish held the behaviour of most people in a stance as stiff as a hymn-book. Religion became a passion. Nonconformity burned up surplus energy like a gas-vent at a colliery—Sunday worship, Sunday schools, Pleasant Sunday Afternoons, prayer-meetings, Men's Bible-class, Women's Bright Hour, Watch Night, Harvest Festivals, Sunday School Anniversary processions, *Messiah*, choir suppers, concerts. The singing even burst out of the chapels into Male Voice Choirs and amateur operatic societies and all the fierce, inter-town warfare of the competitive musical festivals, which, in the late 1930s, were to provide the first training-ground for Kathleen Ferrier.

Sport was equally serious and pugnacious. A good fifty years after the game my father used to argue about a try that put Millom out of the Northern Rugby League Cup. Cricket demanded a self-surrender like that of a religious conversion—you "heard a call" to be a slow bowler—and every league match held the crowd intent as at prayer or as exaltant when they won as those Saved by the Salvation Army.

That was the world of my boyhood and it continued, not greatly changed, until 1939. Today the savage local loyalties and prejudices are fast dying out. The cricket teams, flush on licensed club bars, can now engage colonial test-match players as their professionals, but they can scarcely draw a decent gate. The young people of present-day West Cumberland do not think of themselves as being different from those of similar age and class in, say, Sheffield or even London, nor do they wish to be different. Most of the new industries, unlike coal and iron mining, might quite just as well have been sited in any other part of industrial England. The new prosperity has certainly made life more comfortable in Cumberland, but it has also made it more ordinary. Some of the Cumbrian-ness has already been rubbed off and more undoubtedly will be.

The West Coast Renaissance

That the West Coast began to revive towards the end of the

thirties was due in the first place to the work of the Cumberland Development Council, under the leadership of Jack Adams (later Lord Adams of Ennerdale) and in the second place to the War. I remember the afternoon of the mid-thirties—I think it was a Wednesday—when my father, who was then chairman of the Millom Chamber of Trade, attended a meeting at Workington and came back saying that they had decided to set up a committee to attract new industries to the district. He was not very hopeful, nor, at that time, did there seem much reason for hope. But, thanks to the almost fanatical persistence of Jack Adams, factories at last began to be opened in the area.

Some of them were small businesses, set up in converted Drill Halls, markets and disused chapels, employing for the most part, girls between the age of school and the age of marriage. Others were on a much larger scale, owned or managed, many of them, by refugees and exiles from the continent, who introduced industrial techniques new to England. In the last thirty-five years a few of the products of the new West Cumberland have become well known to almost every one.

The War, of course, brought a revival in iron and steel and in coal, but the future of both these industries is unsettled, and mining, in particular, is almost dead. The War also brought munition works, T.N.T. and shell-filling factories, and when these were no longer needed the site of one of them, Windscale, became the site of the world's first atomic power plant.

I am not one who thinks that the splitting of the atom is likely to be a boon to mankind, but Sellafield (which is how Cumberland people always refer to the atomic station) has played a great part in the west coast revival. It has given new jobs to the men of the worked-out mining towns; it offers careers for local boys with technical and scientific training; and it has produced our most impressive industrial architecture since the blast-furnaces. Above all, it has given the once-isolated West Cumbrians a sense of being in the front line of the twentieth century.[1] We have already paid for this dubious honour by pouring our milk down the drains during the radio-active leak of some years ago; we may pay at a higher price in the future. But, at present, Sellafield helps to keep more than just the Geiger counters ticking.

Most of our new industries are not particularly Cumbrian.

[1] See: Stuart Sinclair: *Windscale* (G. Newnes, 1960).

The church at Kirkby Stephen

They came to the district because men needed work and not because the nature or climate or resources of Cumberland specially favoured silks, plastics, nylon, leather, hats, underwear, boots and shoes or the like. Yet one important industry did come right out of the native rock and gave a new meaning to mining in the centre of the old mining area. This is Marchon,[1] a chemical manufacturing firm, founded in 1939, which moved to White-haven during the War after having been bombed out of London. It started in a small way, making firelighters, and turned, later, to the development of synthetic detergents. Round about 1950, Marchon began to concentrate attention on raw materials for the detergent industry, especially on the phosphates which are ob-tained from phosphate rock and sulphuric acid. But sulphur, needed to produce the sulphuric acid, was very scarce in the early 1950s and imports had to be paid for in dollars that were even scarcer. And then—as so often in the history of mining—luck changed the shape of the future. For the Marchon Factory at Sandwith, between Whitehaven and St. Bees, was known to be standing over a vast deposit of anhydrite (calcium sulphate) that lies five hundred feet down and consists, it is estimated, of hundreds of millions of tons—perhaps thousands of millions. By now it is some two million tons less, most of the extracted rock having gone to produce sulphuric acid and, as a by-product, cement. The anhydrite plant, perched on the edge of the Fleswick Bay cliffs, looks the wrong colour for Cumberland, talcum-pow-dered like a bathed baby in the dust of the detergent factory next door. All the same, the whole industry comes straight out of the rock—as Cumbrian as rum butter.

The revival does not mean that West Cumberland will be prosperous for ever more. Steel and iron and coal are passing through a bad patch, Sellafield is keeping on fewer builders and labourers, and many men are out of work. The future cannot be separated from that of the industrial North as a whole, but, in comparison with the dole days, new life, new health, and a new cheerfulness have undoubtedly come into the district. The sense of isolation is dying out, and so also are many of the old traditions,

[1] The firm's name, which is compounded of parts of the names of its two founders, Frank Schon and Fred Marzillier, is intended to be pronounced "March On", but West Cumberland people invariably render it as "Marshon".

The main street in Appleby

the fierce local patriotism, the oddness, the almost unique-ness of the Cumberland working towns.

There are other changes, too. Sellafield brought to the area a large number of trained specialists who might have been expected to form a clique, a sophisticated *élite* among the provincial hobble-dehoys. In fact, many of them have shown the greatest appreciation of their new environment, turning to it as walkers, rock-climbers, under-water swimmers, bird watchers, botanists or historians. So long as Sellafield does not try to claim Wastwater as a reservoir the men of the atomic station are likely to remain enthusiastic champions and defenders of the fells.

The revival also brought to West Cumberland many foreign industrialists and technicians—some of them refugees from the Nazis—whose assimilation into the local scene has been less easy. This is a topic rarely mentioned in public though continually turned over in private. The new-comers were inevitably looked on with suspicion. Because many of them made money quickly, they were looked on with envy. Some of them, feeling, no doubt, that the district owed much to them, behaved with some condescension towards the people who had received them. It seemed for a while that there had come into power a new managing and employing class with no roots in Cumberland and with little in common with the men they employed. This phase is now passing over. The foreign names are beginning to sound familiar and their owners—often married to local girls—are rearing children who seem entirely English in speech and outlook. Once again Cumberland has absorbed an invasion as, three to four hundred years ago, it absorbed the German and Flemish miners.

And, as in those former times, it is the richer for the blood transfusion. Economics and industry apart, perhaps our greatest debt to the immigrants is for the Rosehill Theatre, set up by Sir Nicholas Sekers in the grounds of his house near Moresby. The building was originally a barn, and has been converted into a small concert hall of almost over-indulgent elegance and comfort. To this theatre have come soloists and chamber groups who would have been received with enthusiasm in any part of the world. Benjamin Britten has conducted *The Turn of the Screw* and there have been visits from the Royal Shakespeare and other drama companies. The seats are not cheap and it is not always easy to get in, yet people come from all corners of Cumberland and Westmorland,

travelling back over the black fell roads, often in mist and darkness. To some of us, especially those who live a good way from
the theatre, a visit can only be a rare treat, but it is nearly always
one to be remembered with immense pleasure.

Of course, Rosehill has been criticized. It is too expensive. It
caters too much for a boiled shirt[1] and cocktail public—one wonders, at times, if members of the audience would have attended
the same series of concerts if they had been held in a Methodist
Sunday school, price 3/6. Rosehill, in fact, aims rather too much
at being fashionable. So far, it has scarcely tried to make itself
much of a centre for local arts, talents and interests, and this seems
to me to be a pity. But for what it has done—for giving us the
opportunity, for instance, of hearing the Amadeus Quartet per-
form the Beethoven Opus 132—we owe Sir Nicholas and his little
theatre our large and delighted gratitude.

[1] But I do not wear a boiled shirt and no one, as yet, has tried to turn me out.

XI

THE FUTURE OF THE LAKES

WHAT is going to happen to the Lakes?

Let me say, first of all, what I do not want to happen. I do not want the Lakes to be turned into a museum. I do not want to see them smothered in good taste, embalmed in admiration. I do not want the dales to be bought up and managed by townsmen until the local people become entirely dependent on town money and live like Red Indians in a National Park reservation. I do not want to see the clutter and coarseness of farm life cleaned up and white-washed into the prettiness of the week-end cottage. I do not want the Lakes to be transformed into a series of coloured transparencies, where not a wall nor a roof strikes the wrong tone and the view is as neat as a postage stamp. I do not want to see the fells become like Arthur's Seat in Edinburgh—preserved, patrolled, tarmacked, tidied, molly-coddled and dead.

Twenty-five years ago I felt that the one thing to be done about the Lakes was to leave them alone. Let the farms have their electricity; let the villages have their factories if they want them. Don't complain about quarries; don't protest against mineral workings. Give the dalesman a chance to go on living and making a living, and to stay more or less independent of the tourist, and the landscape will look after itself as it has done for thousands of years. Don't interfere. Don't stifle the life of a dale community for the sake of saving a view. Heaven preserve us—I said—from the preservers. And I made strong criticisms of the Friends of the Lake District, even though their secretary, the late H. H. Symonds, was a man whose friendship was an honour and whose company, a delight.

Today—though I still think I was right—I no longer complain about most of the activities of the Friends; indeed, I have become a Friend myself. Why has my attitude changed?

In fact, it has not changed at all: it is society which has changed. The Lakes are no longer a place apart. Post-war prosperity, extra spending money and the vast spawning of cars have brought urban

England roaring up to our borders. It is not just that immense numbers of people now come to the Lakes, for the fells are big enough to take more without being crowded. (Though, of course, it is going to be increasingly difficult to provide all the car-parks, caravan sites and holiday accommodation which will be needed.) It is rather that tourism is becoming the dominant industry of the area. At one time the tourists were received in farms, villages and towns which made their living in their own way—from sheep, wool, quarries, mines and the like. They were glad of the extra money from the visitor but they did not depend upon him. Today the visitor is beginning to own the place and, if we are not careful, the whole area will be turned into one vast holiday camp. Nobody wants this to happen—least of all the visitor who comes to the Lakes because he likes them as they are. But the ruthless pressure of profit pushes us continually in that direction.

It is against this kind of commercial exploitation that the Friends of the Lake District and the National Park Planning Board now have to fight. Such preposterous proposals as a glass-bottomed floating ballroom on Ullswater or a cable-car railway to the top of Helvellyn are fairly easily laughed out of likelihood. But there are others, less objectionable in themselves, which threaten to turn the Lakes into a kind of mountain Pleasure Beach—speed boats, water-skiing, unnecessary motor roads over the passes, juke-boxes, skittle-alleys, garish hotels, road-houses and cafés, some of which have already reached the stomach-turning point in hideous and incongruous décor. It is the prime aim of the National Parks to preserve the countryside for the visitor, but there is a danger that the visitor will destroy just what has been preserved for him.

Planning can certainly help to ease out some of the problems. It can see that caravan sites, car-parks and the like are reasonably inconspicuous. It might also try to persuade visitors that it is often more convenient to stay a little outside the popular central area, and that it is always better to come outside the central holiday months. A spreading of the tourist trade over a greater part of the year would be to the benefit of both the trade and the tourist.

But, of course, the only real defence against the erosion of tourism is the survival of a living community, long-rooted in the locality, making its own way and at least partially independent of the visitor. I think that all that can be done should be done to help the hill farmer, both by the Ministry of Agriculture and by the local authorities. Where the interests of the farmer conflict with those of the tourist, the farmer should be given first con-sideration every time. I think that the Planning Board should try to see that life is made practicable and reasonably profitable for the men who still choose to work in the dales. They should get electricity and water; their roads should be good enough for tradesmen's vans and other services. There should be good bus transport, good schools, village halls and the like. I should like to see the Friends as anxious to encourage industries in the dale villages as they are (quite rightly) to discourage unsightly camps on the lake sides. And I would be ready to accept even a certain amount of ugliness, if necessary, in order that the dales might be kept alive.

Electricity is a relevant case. If the cables can be taken under-ground, all well and good. But if not, then it is better that they should go overground, even if this spoils the view, than that the man who lives in the dales all the year round should be deprived of a service which the townsman takes for granted. In this parti-cular instance, the problem is largely one of cost. So that it seems essential that the Planning Board should have funds to compensate the Post Office, the farmers, the local builders and others who are willing to take extra trouble and spend extra money to save the landscape. In the case of Borrowdale, the Friends of the Lake District offered £5,000 towards the cost of laying the electricity cables underground. That cost ought really to be borne by the nation. If we can afford to spend half a million on a picture that very few people will ever see, then we can afford to spend a little extra on a landscape that has brought pleasure to hundreds of thousands. And, if it comes to that, what is the cost of interior decoration at some of the royal residences?

The new council houses at Hawkshead, Coniston and elsewhere present a similar case. They are—at least at Hawkshead—tucked nicely out of sight, but no one could call them prepossessing. There are hundreds of old cow-sheds and tumble-down slate walls that are far more pleasing to the eye. Yet they are entirely necessary, for as the dale cottages fall vacant they are eagerly bought and reconditioned by retired townsmen. The results of the re-building are often comfortable and tasteful and outwardly at harmony with the scene, but they are far beyond the pocket of the local labourer, who will be driven out of the district altogether if he cannot find somewhere to live at a reasonable rent. Council houses are the obvious answer, but councils cannot afford to spend more than they must and are often impatient of criticism or protest. In such cases, a money grant from the Planning Board might make the difference between a house that needs to be hidden away and one that can be looked at as well as lived in. The important thing is that whenever possible—and it is nearly always possible—new buildings should be of the local stone, which not only means that they soon settle into the landscape but also that work is given to local quarrymen and stone-masons. The extra cost goes into the pockets of the men who most need it.

The Planning Board does not only lack funds; it lacks power. Of course, when it is a matter of rejecting the plans for a proposed bungalow or a harmless industrial project like that to open a small deposit of diatomaceous earth near Skeggles Water, then the board is able to act. But over the really great threats to the District it seems to be helpless. When Manchester wanted to turn Ullswater into a reservoir it was not the Planning Board that saved it but the eloquence of Lord Birkett in the House of Lords.[1]

If the National Park policy is to have any point at all, then surely the Planning Board should have a final veto against municipal or government exploitation. Too often the proclamation of a park is followed by the setting up of atomic stations, missile ranges, military training grounds, hydro-electric schemes or reservoirs, so that few parts of our District are entirely safe. It is doubtful if Manchester has put aside all hopes of Ullswater, while Windscale is said to have its eye on Wastwater. Bannisdale—though reprieved along with Ullswater—is not forgotten, and work is well on the way on the dam in Wet Sleddale.

Then there are the road makers. Before the direction of the Carnforth to Penrith section of the M6 was decided upon, surveyors are said to have considered Longsleddale as an alternative to Shap. Such a choice would have been disastrous. As it is, the new motorway passes through country which, apart from the Lune Gorge, is open enough to accept it without undue disfigurement.

[1] February 1962. Lord Birkett died very soon after making this last triumphant appeal for the defence, and, in gratitude for his efforts, a hill near Ullswater is now named Birkett Fell.

Nevertheless, though the motorway provides quicker access to Scotland and reduces traffic congestion in Kendal, Penrith and Carlisle, it has done little to relieve the shockingly over-crowded Ambleside-Grasmere-Keswick road. Nearly everyone in Furness and West Cumberland thinks that the M6 should have been routed around Morecambe Bay and along the coast, to relieve the Lakes of traffic and give stimulus to industrial Cumberland. Unfortunately, the roads do not come within the powers of the National Park but those of the various County Councils and the Ministry of Transport. This is precisely the kind of dichotomy that threatens to ruin the Lakes. For the two parts of the region—industrial and rural—are inseparably one, and the Park Planners will not be able to plan at all unless they are closely linked with all the other planning authorities concerned. You cannot divide the future of the area into little parcels and look after one at a time. It is no good saying, "We'll save Ullswater and Langdale Pikes, and let Whitehaven, Egremont and Millom stew in their own juice." A thriving West Cumberland and a prosperous ring of market towns in Westmorland and North Lancashire are essential if the Lakes are to retain anything of independence and dignity. Let industrial Cumberland decay, and the National Park will become no more than a convalescent home for a sick urban civilization.

INDEX